# Cultivating Community
## A Business Leader's Guide to Growth Through Giving
### Kevin Wheeler

# Contents

# Dedication

Embarking on crafting this book on reciprocity in business has been a profound experience, filled with introspection, learning, and invaluable insights. This journey is deeply enriched by the support and inspiration from those around me, especially those whose belief in my vision has been unwavering.

At the core of this journey, illuminating the path with grace and wisdom, was my very best friend, Scott Kingslien. Scott departed from us too soon, a noble soul who faced life's ultimate challenge without forewarning. This book is dedicated to him to honor a friend whose support knew no bounds. Despite his cautious approach to the practice of reciprocity in business, his support for me never wavered. He backed me not out of obligation but from a place of genuine kindness and belief in my aspirations.

In dedicating this book to Scott, I celebrate a person who, in essence, personified the very principles of reciprocity I delve into. He may have approached the concept with caution, yet he lived out the values of reciprocal giving in his relationships with others, his generosity, and his steadfast support. Scott was the embodiment of reciprocity's spirit before this book's conception, living out its principles in his everyday actions.

To Scott, my gratitude is boundless. This book aims not only to explore the potential of reciprocity in the business world but also to stand as a testament to the impact of meaningful relationships and the profound influence of those who support us with conviction and love.

Scott, this book is for you. It is interwoven with your spirit and legacy, a silent yet powerful reminder of your influence. May your essence continue to inspire and guide us through these pages, showcasing the strength in true support, the beauty of questioning, and the incomparable value of friendship.

For everyone who turns these pages, I hope you find professional inspiration and a reflection of the principles of friendship, support, and reciprocity that Scott Kingslien exemplified. Here's to our collective journey toward growth, understanding, and mutual success in business and in life.

# 1
# The Power of Giving

I N THE HEART OF every aspiring leader lies the power to transform not just their own life but also the lives of those they aim to serve. My journey to understanding this transformative power was not born out of conventional success stories but through embracing the essence of giving, even when faced with diversity and adversity. This story, my story, begins in a small town where my African-American stepfather and I navigated the challenges of racial prejudice. It was here, amidst ridicule and threats, that I learned the value of gratitude and the profound impact of servant leadership.

Growing up, I learned to navigate the rough waters of prejudice and misunderstanding, not with bitterness, but with a reflective gratitude for the myriad ways life had enriched me. This mindset, nurtured through trials, became my beacon, guiding me toward a leadership style centered on service and reciprocity. Traditional leadership models, preoccupied with self-advancement and organizational success, seemed limiting compared to the boundless potential of serving others. By embracing servant leadership, I aimed to transform the workplaces I was part of and lay the groundwork for my entrepreneurial dreams.

"No one has ever become poor by giving," Anne Frank once said. This quote resonated with me through my formative years and ventures into the corporate world and entrepreneurship. The challenges I faced, from building trust within my teams to overcoming the gnawing doubts of impostor syndrome, were monumental. Yet, the philosophy of reciprocity, the belief in the power of giving, became my beacon of hope and my strategy for unlocking business growth.

The transformation was palpable. By prioritizing the well-being and success of those around me, I fostered a culture of generosity and cooperation and unlocked new avenues for growth and innovation. This journey has taught me that the essence of leadership lies not in the accumulation of personal accolades but in the ability to create a positive impact on the lives of others.

In this chapter, "The Power of Giving: Unlocking Business Growth Through Reciprocity," we will explore how the act of giving and the principle of reciprocity can be leveraged as critical drivers for business success and leadership excellence. Our journey will not just be theoretical; it will be grounded in practical wisdom, engaging storytelling, and the invaluable lessons learned from personal experiences and those of renowned businesses that have thrived on these principles.

1. **Understanding Reciprocity in Business:** We'll delve into reciprocity and its pivotal role in fostering mutually beneficial relationships that can drive growth and foster a culture of trust and loyalty among

partners, customers, and stakeholders.

2. **The Science Behind Giving:** Here, I'll discuss the psychological and sociological studies that support the benefits of reciprocity in business, demonstrating how this understanding can serve as a foundation for trust, reliability, and long-term success.

3. **Case Studies:** We will examine successful businesses like Apple, Nordstrom, and Ritz Carlton that have thrived on reciprocal practices, drawing lessons from their strategies and approaches to cultivating a culture of giving and mutual respect.

4. **Building a Reciprocity-Focused Mindset:** I'll provide practical tips and strategies for incorporating a philosophy of reciprocity into everyday business operations, from leadership practices to company-wide initiatives emphasizing collaboration, generosity, and mutual support.

Through these sections, I aim to offer not just insights but actionable steps to embrace and implement the principles of reciprocity in your leadership journey and business practices. Whether navigating the corporate environment or stepping out to build your own business, the power of giving and the practice of servant leadership can be transformative. It's about shifting the focus from "I" to "we," from personal gain to collective success, and from doubts to unwavering confidence in your ability to lead and inspire.

As we embark on this journey together, remember that the essence of leadership is not just about achieving personal success but about making a positive impact on the lives of others. It's about building strong, cohesive teams and creating a work environment that fosters growth, loyalty, and a shared vision for success. Join me as we unveil the pathways to purposeful entrepreneurship and leadership through the power of giving.

## Understanding Reciprocity in Business

At its core, the concept of reciprocity in business is about fostering a cycle of mutual respect and benefit. This principle has guided me through every step of my leadership journey. When I first stepped into the manager role, I carried with me the aspirations of climbing the corporate ladder and a deep-seated belief in the power of giving. This belief was rooted in my early life experiences, where I learned that through adversity, the true measure of one's character is not just how one rises but how one lifts others in their ascent.

Understanding reciprocity in business is akin to understanding the language of growth and sustainability. It's about recognizing that every interaction, every transaction, is an opportunity to build a bridge, to create a connection that transcends the immediate exchange. My early days were marked by a relentless pursuit of becoming a subject matter expert, not for the accolades or recognition, but for the opportunity it presented to give back—to share knowledge, to mentor, and to guide my team towards collective success.

This journey was not without its challenges. The corporate world, often characterized by its cutthroat competition and relentless pursuit of profit, sometimes seemed at odds with the principles of servant leadership and reciprocity that I deeply valued. Yet, amidst these apparent contradictions, the true essence of reciprocity began to shine through. It was about demonstrating through actions, not just words, that the company's success was intrinsically linked to the well-being of its people.

At its core, reciprocity is about giving and receiving, but not in the transactional sense we so often encounter. It's about fostering relationships where generosity and cooperation lead to mutual benefits, creating a cycle of positivity that propels growth and success.

The impact of embracing reciprocity was profound. By fostering an environment where every team member felt valued and heard, where their contributions were recognized and their growth nurtured, we began to see a shift. Productivity increased, not just in output but in the quality of work and the innovation it spurred. The teams I led were not just groups of individuals working towards a common goal; they were a cohesive unit bound by a shared sense of purpose and trust.

In my early days as a leader, I observed a common pitfall: the relentless pursuit of personal or organizational gain without regard for the broader community or the needs of others. While this approach might yield short-term gains, it often fails to build the trust and loyalty essential for long-term success. I challenged this norm, guided by the wisdom that "No one has ever become poor by giving." I focused on how my actions and decisions could benefit my immediate goals and the aspirations and well-being of those around me.

But how does one cultivate such an environment? It begins with the simple act of giving. In my case, it was about giving time to listen to my team's concerns and aspirations, understand their challenges, and work collaboratively towards solutions. It was about giving recognition, openly acknowledging individuals' hard work and achievements, and showing appreciation for their efforts.

Moreover, giving opportunities and creating avenues for growth and development allowed each team member to realize their potential. This approach to leadership, grounded in reciprocity, empowered my team and allowed me to grow as a leader. It taught me that authentic leadership is not about wielding power but about sharing it, not about leading from the front but walking alongside those you aim to lead.

The statistics speak for themselves. A 2020 study by Cone Communications highlighted that 87% of consumers are likelier to purchase a product from a company that advocates for an issue they care about. This underscores the broader implications of reciprocity in business—it's not just about internal team dynamics but about how a company positions itself globally. By embodying the principles of giving and service, a company can build a brand that is successful, respected, and admired.

Reflecting on my journey, it's clear that the power of reciprocity in business is not just a philosophical ideal but a practical strategy for growth and success. It's about building a legacy of leadership that is measured not by the wealth it accumulates but by the lives it touches and the positive changes it inspires. As we move forward in this chapter, I invite you to join me in exploring the science behind giving, the case studies of successful businesses that have thrived on reciprocal practices, and the practical steps you can take to incorporate this philosophy into your daily operations.

Through understanding reciprocity in business, we unlock the potential to transform not just our organizations but the very nature of leadership itself. It's a journey towards creating a more connected, collaborative, and compassionate business world where the power of giving becomes the cornerstone of success.

## The Science Behind Giving

Embarking on the path of leadership and entrepreneurship, I've always been fascinated by the forces that shape our interactions and decisions. Among these, the principle of giving and its impact on business dynamics holds a special place. It's not just a moral choice but a strategic one underpinned by a wealth of psychological and sociological research. The science behind giving offers a window into the human psyche, revealing how acts of generosity and reciprocity can lead to mutual success and fulfillment.

In my quest to understand this more profoundly, I turned to studies and theories that explain why we are intrinsically motivated to reciprocate when someone does us a favor or extends a gesture of goodwill. This exploration led me to the concept of social exchange theory, which posits that human relationships are formed by using a subjective cost-benefit analysis and comparing alternatives. Simply put, when we give, we do not just do so out of altruism; we subconsciously anticipate a form of return, not necessarily immediate or material, but a strengthening of bonds, trust, and cooperation.

The implications of this for business are profound. As leaders, when we adopt a giving mindset, we're not just investing in the welfare of our teams and customers; we're setting the stage for a reciprocal exchange that can yield dividends beyond the tangible. A study that resonated with me deeply, published by the Harvard Business Review, highlighted how leaders who give their time, resources, and attention freely often see a return in the form of increased loyalty, productivity, and innovation from their teams.

This science of giving extends beyond internal dynamics to

how businesses interact with their customers and the wider community. The 2020 study by Cone Communications, which found that 87% of consumers are more likely to support companies that advocate for issues they care about, is a testament to the power of reciprocity in shaping consumer behavior. It's a clear indication that businesses that give back and engage in socially responsible practices build a strong brand identity and foster a loyal customer base that values their commitment to the greater good.

Reflecting on my journey, I've seen the truth of these findings firsthand. In my efforts to lead with generosity, prioritize the needs and growth of my team, and engage in community-driven initiatives, I've witnessed how these acts of giving have come full circle. It's not just about the immediate gratification of doing good; it's about creating a culture where giving is woven into the fabric of our daily operations, where each act of generosity sparks another, creating a virtuous cycle of growth and success.

But how do we navigate this path of giving in a business context? It starts with authenticity. In a world where consumers are increasingly savvy and discerning, genuine acts of generosity stand out. It's about more than just corporate social responsibility as a checkbox; it's about embedding these values into the core of your business strategy, making giving a part of your brand's DNA.

Moreover, the science of giving emphasizes the importance of empathy and understanding. By putting ourselves in the shoes of those we aim to serve, whether our employees, customers, or community members, we can better identify how to make a meaningful impact. This empathy-driven approach to giving enhances our relationships and drives innovation, as we're continually pushed to think outside the box to meet the needs of those around us.

As we delve into the stories of businesses that have thrived on these principles in the next section, remember that the science behind giving is not just about understanding the mechanics of reciprocity. It's about embracing the essence of generosity and recognizing that in the act of giving, we open ourselves up to receiving not just material success but the deeper fulfillment that comes from positively impacting the world around us.

Understanding the science behind giving has been transformative for me. It has shifted my perspective from viewing leadership as a position of power to seeing it as an opportunity to serve and uplift others. As we move forward, let's carry with us the knowledge that the power of giving is not just a philosophical ideal but a scientifically supported strategy for building more robust, more resilient businesses and communities.

## Case Studies - Thriving on Reciprocal Practices

The journey through giving and reciprocity in business brings us to a pivotal exploration—how do these principles manifest in the real world, shaping the destinies of companies and their communities? As I delve into the case studies of Apple, Nordstrom, and Ritz Carlton, it's clear that their success is not merely a result of innovative products or superior customer service. Instead, it's deeply rooted in their commitment to reciprocal practices, where giving and serving form the cornerstone of their operations.

**Apple:** The story of Apple is not just a narrative of technological innovation; it's a testament to the power of creating ecosystems where every stakeholder feels valued and involved. Apple's approach to reciprocity extends beyond its products to customer service and community engagement. By fostering a culture of listening and responding to customer feedback, Apple has built a loyal community of users who feel deeply connected to the brand. This sense of belonging and loyalty directly results from Apple's commitment to giving back, whether through unparalleled product support or initiatives that prioritize customer privacy and environmental sustainability. My reflections on Apple's success underscore the importance of reciprocal relationships in building a brand that people trust and advocate for.

**Nordstrom:** Nordstrom's reputation for exceptional customer service is legendary, but the company's unwavering commitment to the principle of giving lies at the heart of this distinction. Nordstrom empowers its employees to go above and beyond in serving customers, creating a culture where acts of kindness and generosity are encouraged and expected. This philosophy of giving or putting the customer's needs first has cemented Nordstrom's status as a retail leader. My interactions with their brand have always inspired me, reaffirming my belief in the transformative power of service and reciprocity in fostering brand loyalty and customer satisfaction.

**Ritz Carlton:** In the hospitality industry, where service is the currency of success, Ritz Carlton stands out for its dedication to creating unforgettable experiences for its guests. This commitment is rooted in a deep-seated belief in the value of servant leadership and reciprocity. Ritz Carlton's motto, "We are Ladies and Gentlemen serving Ladies and Gentlemen," encapsulates this ethos, emphasizing respect, dignity, and the desire to give back in every interaction. My observations of Ritz Carlton's operations reveal meticulous attention to detail and a genuine passion for service, proving that when businesses prioritize giving and reciprocity, they can achieve unparalleled excellence in customer experience.

Reflecting on these case studies, it's evident that the principles of giving and reciprocity are not just abstract concepts but actionable strategies that can drive business growth and success. These companies exemplify how integrating a culture of service and generosity into business operations can lead to a loyal customer base, motivated employees, and a strong, sustainable brand.

As I ponder the lessons from Apple, Nordstrom, and Ritz Carlton, I'm reminded of the countless ways in which my leadership journey has been influenced by these principles.

From the early days of navigating the challenges of diversity and adversity to my ongoing efforts to build cohesive, trusting teams, the philosophy of servant leadership and reciprocity has been a guiding light.

In the next section, "Building a Reciprocity-Focused Mindset," we will explore practical tips for incorporating these principles into daily operations. This journey through the science of giving and the real-world success stories of businesses that have thrived on reciprocal practices is a powerful reminder of the transformative potential of leadership rooted in generosity and service.

Let us carry forward the insights and inspirations from these case studies as we continue to unlock the pathways to purposeful entrepreneurship and effective leadership through the power of giving.

## Building a Reciprocity-Focused Mindset

Embarking on this journey of leadership and entrepreneurship and, most importantly, giving has taught me invaluable lessons about the transformative power of a reciprocity-focused mindset. Drawing inspiration from the success stories of Apple, Nordstrom, and Ritz Carlton, it's clear that the path to sustainable business growth and effective leadership is paved with acts of generosity, empathy, and mutual respect. In this section, I will share practical tips that have not only shaped my approach to leadership but can also guide you in weaving reciprocity into the fabric of your business operations.

## Fostering an Environment of Generosity and Support

The first step towards building a reciprocity-focused mindset is fostering an environment where generosity and support are encouraged and celebrated. This begins with leading by example. I've learned that my actions as a leader have a profound impact on the culture of my team. By prioritizing the well-being of my team members, actively listening to their ideas and concerns, and recognizing their contributions, I've cultivated an atmosphere of trust and mutual respect.

**Practical Tip:** Start team meetings with a 'gratitude round,' during which each member shares something they are thankful for, whether professional or personal. This simple practice can enhance team cohesion and foster a positive work environment.

## Empowering Through Delegation and Trust

Empowerment is a critical component of a reciprocity-focused mindset. I've discovered that delegation is not just about distributing tasks but about entrusting your team with responsibilities that challenge and grow their capabilities. This trust encourages a sense of ownership and pride in their work, leading to higher engagement and productivity.

**Practical Tip:** Identify opportunities for team members to lead projects or initiatives that align with their strengths and interests. This will not only boost their confidence but also demonstrate your trust in their abilities.

## Encouraging Open Communication and Transparency

Open communication and transparency are the cornerstones of building reciprocal relationships. I've prioritized maintaining an open-door policy, encouraging my team to share their ideas, concerns, and feedback freely. This transparency fosters a culture of honesty and collaboration, where every team member feels valued and heard.

**Practical Tip:** Implement regular feedback sessions where team members can provide constructive feedback on projects, processes, and management practices. This will improve operations and strengthen the team's sense of belonging and investment in the company's success.

## Giving Back to the Community

A reciprocity-focused mindset extends beyond the confines of the office. It's about recognizing our role and responsibility as business leaders in the broader community. My commitment to giving back, whether through volunteering, philanthropy, or sustainability initiatives, has enriched my personal growth and positively impacted my brand's reputation and customer loyalty.

**Practical Tip:** Partner with local nonprofits or community organizations on projects or events that align with your company's values. This will contribute to the community and enhance team spirit and company culture.

## Measuring Success Beyond Profits

Finally, adopting a reciprocity-focused mindset requires reevaluating how we measure success. While financial performance is undoubtedly important, I've learned to value the intangible aspects of business success, such as employee satisfaction, customer loyalty, and community impact. These metrics are true indicators of a company's sustainability and legacy.

**Practical Tip:** Incorporate non-financial metrics into your business reviews, such as employee engagement scores, customer satisfaction ratings, and community impact assessments. This broader perspective on success can motivate your team and guide your business toward meaningful growth.

In conclusion, building a reciprocity-focused mindset is more than just implementing specific practices; it's about embodying the principles of generosity, empathy, and service in every aspect of leadership and business operations. As we wrap up this chapter, I hope these insights and practical tips inspire you to embrace reciprocity as a strategy and a way of life, paving the way for a more connected, collaborative, and compassionate business world.

## Embracing the Journey Ahead

As we draw this chapter to a close, I reflect on the profound journey of discovery, growth, and transformation that the principles of giving and reciprocity have ushered into my life and leadership. "The Power of Giving: Unlocking Business Growth Through Reciprocity" is more than a chapter title; it's a lived experience and a testament to the boundless potential of embracing generosity, service, and mutual respect as cornerstones of leadership and business success.

## The Essence of Reciprocity in Leadership

My journey, marked by the challenges of diversity and adversity, has been a testament to the resilience of the human spirit and the transformative power of giving. From my early days, grappling with the nuances of servant leadership, to the heights of corporate and entrepreneurial success, the principle of reciprocity has been my guiding light. It has taught me that authentic leadership is not about accumulating power or prestige but the ability to inspire, uplift, and serve others.

## Fostering a Culture of Generosity and Support

Building a reciprocity-focused mindset has been a journey of intentional practice, starting with fostering a culture where generosity and support are encouraged and celebrated. This culture, rooted in the acts of giving time, recognition, and opportunities, has been the foundation of building cohesive, productive teams and establishing a brand that resonates with loyalty and trust.

## Empowering Through Trust and Delegation

The empowerment of my team through trust and delegation has not only facilitated personal and professional growth. Still, it has also reinforced the importance of mutual respect and the value of each individual's contribution. This approach has underscored the belief that leadership is about walking alongside those you lead, sharing the journey of growth and success.

## Commitment to Open Communication and Community Engagement

Open communication and transparency have been pivotal in nurturing an environment of trust and collaboration. At the same time, our commitment to giving back to the community has broadened our perspective, reminding us of our more significant role and responsibility in society's tapestry. These practices have enriched our lives and endeared our brand to customers and stakeholders, creating a legacy of impact and integrity.

## Redefining Success

This journey has also been about redefining success, recognizing that actual achievement lies not in financial metrics alone but in the intangible yet invaluable measures of employee satisfaction, customer loyalty, and community impact. This broader view of success has inspired a more profound sense of purpose and fulfillment, guiding us toward a legacy that transcends the confines of traditional business metrics.

## The Path Ahead

As we embark on the path ahead, armed with the insights and lessons from this chapter, it's clear that the journey of incorporating reciprocity into our leadership and business practices is ongoing. It's a path marked by continuous learning, growth, and the unwavering commitment to serve and give back.

## Five Action Steps to Integrate Reciprocity into Your Leadership Practice

1. **Cultivate a Culture of Gratitude:** Begin each day or meeting by acknowledging and expressing gratitude for the contributions and presence of your team members.

2. **Empower with Trust:** Identify opportunities to delegate meaningful responsibilities to team members, demonstrating your trust and encouraging their growth.

3. **Foster Open Communication:** Implement regular

feedback sessions, creating a safe space for open dialogue and sharing ideas and concerns.

4. **Engage with the Community:** As a team, choose a community project or cause to support, reinforcing the value of giving back and broadening your impact beyond the business.

5. **Measure What Matters:** Expand your definition of success to include non-financial metrics such as employee engagement, customer satisfaction, and community impact, ensuring these are integral to your business review processes.

In closing, the power of giving and the principle of reciprocity have illuminated the path to leadership and business success, revealing that the greatest achievements are those shared in the spirit of generosity and service. Let us carry forward these principles, not just as growth strategies but as beacons of hope and transformation in our journey towards purposeful entrepreneurship and impactful leadership.

As we look to the future, let us embrace the journey ahead with open hearts and minds, ready to unlock the infinite possibilities that lie in the power of giving.

# 2

# Building Trust - The Foundation of Reciprocity

I N THE HEART OF every thriving business lies a silent yet powerful force: trust. It's the invisible glue that binds, the foundation upon which the towering aspirations of companies rest. Imagine, for a moment, the story of a small brick-and-mortar store nestled in the bustling streets of a vibrant city. The owner, a visionary leader, dreams not just of profit but of building a legacy that weaves into the fabric of the community. This is not a tale from a distant past or a line from a motivational movie; it's the reality of businesses striving to scale in a world increasingly interconnected yet divided by skepticism.

The principle of reciprocity stands as a testament to the power of giving to get. It's a concept deeply rooted in our human nature, compelling us to return favors, extend kindness, and build relationships on the bedrock of mutual benefit. In business, this goes beyond the transactional exchanges of goods and services. It's about creating a cycle of goodwill that fosters loyalty and propels growth. But you may wonder, can a business leader harness this ancient principle to navigate the modern marketplace?

Stepping into a quiet room filled with the soft hum of anticipation, I, a seasoned business leader, reflect on the journey that has brought me here. This isn't just another boardroom; it's the culmination of years of striving toward a vision that transcends the conventional success metrics. It's about establishing a legacy of trust, built on the foundation of reciprocity, within the tapestry of business relationships that have defined my career.

In the bustling business world, where transactions and interactions weave a complex web of connections, trust often seems like a fragile thread. Yet, this very thread holds the potential to transform the ordinary into the extraordinary. Drawing inspiration from Stephen R. Covey's profound insight, "Trust is the glue of life. It's the most essential ingredient in effective communication," I've realized that trust isn't just an element of business; it's the cornerstone upon which all successful endeavors are built.

Imagine a moment in a world where business isn't just a series of transactions but a dance of mutual respect and understanding, a harmony of give and take. This is the world I envision for us, where reciprocity isn't just a practice but a principle that guides every decision and interaction. It's about more than just the bottom line; it's about creating a legacy that values relationships as the highest currency.

My journey to this understanding was dynamic. It was filled with moments of reflection, challenges, and revelations that shaped my perspective on the role of trust in business. There was a time when I viewed success through a traditional lens, measuring growth, revenue, and market share achievements. However, a pivotal experience shifted my focus toward the intangible yet invaluable asset of trust.

During a visit to a small, family-owned business, I witnessed the power of reciprocity firsthand. This business thrived not because of aggressive marketing strategies or cutting-edge technology but because of its unwavering commitment to its community. The owners understood their customers' needs and went above and beyond to meet them, fostering a sense of loyalty and support that money couldn't buy. This experience was a revelation, illuminating the path to building lasting success through reciprocity and trust.

As I share this story with you, I invite you to embark on a journey with me that explores the transformative power of trust in business. This chapter will delve into the essence of trust as a business imperative. It will uncover why it's essential for reciprocity and how it forms the foundation upon which mutually beneficial relationships are built. We'll explore strategies for creating authentic connections with customers and partners, tactics for overcoming mistrust, and the undeniable correlation between trust and sustainable business growth.

In the following sections, we'll explore:

1. The role of trust in establishing reciprocity and its impact on business relationships.

2. Practical strategies for creating authentic connections and fostering an environment where trust flourishes.

3. Methods to rebuild trust where it has been eroded, highlighting the importance of transparency and accountability.

4. The direct correlation between trust, customer loyalty, and long-term success illustrates how trust can be a significant differentiator in a competitive marketplace.

As we navigate these topics, I encourage you to reflect on your experiences with trust in your professional journey. Consider the moments when trust made a difference, a leap of faith opened doors to unexpected opportunities, and the bonds of mutual respect and understanding paved the way for success.

As we'll discover, trust is more than just a concept; it's a practice that, when integrated into the very fabric of our businesses, can lead to unparalleled growth and fulfillment. It's about building a legacy that outlives the immediate transaction, creating a ripple effect of positive impact that resonates far beyond our immediate circle.

So, as we turn the page on traditional business practices, let's embrace the promise of reciprocity, guided by the foundational principle of trust. Let's forge a path toward a future where our businesses are thriving and meaningful, leaving a lasting imprint on the world around us.

## Trust as a Business Imperative - Why trust is essential for reciprocity

In exploring trust as the cornerstone of business reciprocity, we delve deeper into why trust is beneficial and essential for reciprocity to flourish. Trust, in its essence, is the belief in the reliability, truth, ability, or strength of someone or something. In a business context, this translates to stakeholders' confidence in a company's commitment to meeting and exceeding expectations, fostering an environment where reciprocal relationships can thrive.

The foundation of trust is built on consistency, integrity, and transparency. When businesses consistently deliver on their promises, act with integrity in all dealings, and maintain transparency in their operations, they lay the groundwork for trust. This trust paves the way for reciprocity, where mutual benefits drive relationships rather than short-term transactions. When grounded in faith, giving to receive transforms customer interactions from mere exchanges to meaningful relationships.

Consider the power of trust in customer relationships. When customers trust a business, they are more likely to return, recommend it to others, and engage in positive word-of-mouth marketing. This is reciprocity in action; the company provides value beyond the transaction, and in return, customers become advocates and loyal supporters. The trust that underpins these relationships is not given lightly; it is earned through consistent, positive experiences and the business's unwavering commitment to its values and customers.

Building this trust requires a deliberate effort to understand and align with customers' needs and expectations. It involves listening to positive or negative feedback and using it to improve. This process of continuous improvement, driven by customer input, strengthens trust over time, making it the most reliable foundation for a reciprocal business model.

Moreover, trust extends beyond customer relationships to encompass all stakeholder interactions, including employees, partners, and the community. Employees who trust their employers are more engaged, productive, and likely to contribute to a positive workplace culture. This, in turn, enhances the company's ability to provide exceptional service, further reinforcing trust with customers and partners. Community trust is equally important, as businesses are seen as responsible, and contributing members of their community benefit from increased goodwill and support.

To operationalize trust as a business imperative, companies can implement several strategies:

1. **Transparent Communication:** Keep stakeholders informed about decisions, changes, and challenges. Transparency fosters trust by demonstrating honesty

and openness.

2. **Integrity in Actions:** Ensure that all actions, from customer interactions to internal decisions, align with the company's values and ethical standards.

3. **Consistent Quality:** Deliver high-quality products and services consistently to build reliability and trust.

4. **Responsiveness:** Quickly address customer and stakeholder issues, concerns, and feedback. Showing that you value their input and are willing to act on it builds trust.

5. **Personalization:** Treat customers and stakeholders as individuals with unique needs and preferences. Personalized interactions show that you value and respect them, further building trust.

Incorporating these strategies into your business practices can create a culture of trust that supports reciprocity. Trust becomes the currency of your business, facilitating exchanges that are not just transactional but transformational. It allows for a deeper connection with stakeholders, fostering an environment where mutual benefits and growth are possible and expected.

In conclusion, trust is the essential ingredient in the recipe for business reciprocity. It is the foundation upon which mutually beneficial relationships are built and sustained. By prioritizing trust, businesses can unlock the full potential of reciprocity, leading to unparalleled growth, loyalty, and success. This chapter has laid the groundwork for understanding the importance of trust in business; the subsequent sections will build on this foundation, exploring strategies for creating authentic connections, overcoming mistrust, and demonstrating the correlation between trust and long-term success.

Are you ready to explore creating authentic connections, the next step in building a trust-based reciprocal business model?

## Creating Authentic Connections - Strategies for genuine engagement with customers and partners.

Moving deeper into the essence of building a trust-based business landscape, we now focus on creating authentic connections—strategies that foster genuine engagement and serve as the bedrock for long-term relationships with customers and partners. Authenticity in business interactions is not just a best practice; it's necessary in today's marketplace, where consumers and partners value transparency and sincerity above all else.

Creating authentic connections with customers and partners is a pivotal step toward fostering an environment of trust and reciprocity in business. This section delves into the strategies and methodologies companies can employ to genuinely engage with their stakeholders, laying the groundwork for lasting relationships built on mutual respect and understanding.

Creating authentic connections starts with understanding that every customer and partner interaction is an opportunity to demonstrate your company's values and commitment to more than just profit. These connections are built on active listening, empathy, and the personalized experiences that come from truly understanding the unique needs and preferences of those you work with.

**Active Listening and Empathy:** One of the most powerful tools in building authentic connections is listening actively and empathizing with others. This means giving undivided attention to customers and partners, understanding their perspectives, and responding in a way that shows genuine care for their concerns. Active listening and empathy contribute to feeling valued and understood, which is fundamental in establishing trust and reciprocity.

**Personalized Experiences:** In an era where customization is vital, offering customized experiences can significantly enhance the authenticity of your connections. Tailoring your products, services, and communications to meet the individual needs of your customers and partners demonstrates that you recognize and value their uniqueness. This could be as simple as remembering a customer's preferences in your interactions or as complex as customizing a service to address a specific business challenge a partner faces.

**Transparency and Consistent Communication:** Another cornerstone of authentic connections is transparency. Being open about your business practices, successes, and failures makes your company relatable and trustworthy. Consistent communication, whether through regular updates, newsletters, or social media engagement, keeps stakeholders in the loop and fosters a sense of inclusion and partnership.

**Storytelling:** Sharing the stories behind your products, services, and company values can also create stronger, more authentic connections. Stories resonate personally and can convey your company's mission, vision, and values in a way that facts and figures cannot. They provide a narrative that people can connect emotionally, making your business more memorable and relatable.

**Engaging in Meaningful Community Involvement:** Authentic connections extend beyond direct business interactions. Engaging in community service and support initiatives demonstrates your commitment to the broader social good, reinforcing the sincerity of your business values. This engagement should be genuine and aligned with your company's mission rather than a superficial attempt at publicity.

Implementing these strategies requires a shift in mindset from viewing customers and partners as mere transactions to recognizing them as essential contributors to your business's ecosystem. Building authentic connections creates a foundation of trust that encourages mutual support and reciprocity. This environment attracts new customers and partners and nurtures existing relationships, leading to a community of advocates who believe in your business and its values.

In practice, creating authentic connections might involve conducting regular customer feedback sessions to understand their needs better, developing a transparent pricing model that explains costs and benefits clearly, or implementing a customer recognition program that celebrates milestones and achievements. These actions contribute to a culture of authenticity, trust, and reciprocity, paving the way for long-term business success.

As we continue cultivating trust through authenticity, we must remember that authentic connections are not a one-time achievement but a continuous effort. It requires consistent dedication to listening, understanding, and responding to the needs of those you do business with in a way that reflects your core values and commitment to their success.

In the next section, we will explore overcoming mistrust, an inevitable challenge in any business landscape, and how the principles of trust and authenticity can be leveraged to rebuild and strengthen relationships even when trust has been compromised.

Are you ready to move forward and delve into the strategies for overcoming mistrust, an essential step in reinforcing the foundation of trust and reciprocity in business relationships?

## Overcoming Mistrust - Tactics to rebuild trust where it's been lost.

Navigating the murky waters of mistrust in the business realm requires a steadfast commitment to integrity, transparency, and genuine efforts to rebuild confidence. Overcoming mistrust is a testament to a business's resilience and unwavering dedication to its core values and stakeholders.

Mistrust, often resulting from unmet expectations, broken promises, or miscommunications, can erode the foundational trust that reciprocity relies on. Yet, it also presents an opportunity to address issues head-on, rebuild stronger connections, and demonstrate commitment to your values and stakeholders.

**Acknowledging and Addressing the Issue:** The first step in overcoming mistrust is recognizing that an issue exists. This involves open, honest communication and a willingness to listen to grievances without defensiveness. Understanding the root cause of mistrust from the perspective of those affected is crucial. It sets the stage for genuine reconciliation efforts and shows you value the relationship enough to work through difficulties.

**Transparent Action Plan:** Once issues have been acknowledged, developing a clear, actionable plan to address them is vital. This plan should include specific steps to rectify the situation, timelines for when actions will be taken, and clear goals for the resolution process. Transparency in this plan demonstrates your commitment to making things right and allows for accountability, providing stakeholders with a roadmap to track progress.

**Consistent Communication:** Consistent communication is critical throughout the process of overcoming mistrust. Regular updates about the actions being taken, adjustments to the plan as needed, and open forums for feedback help maintain a dialogue. This ongoing communication ensures that stakeholders feel heard and involved in the process, reinforcing the sense of partnership and mutual respect.

**Genuine Apology and Restitution:** When appropriate, offering a sincere apology and making restitution can significantly impact healing and rebuilding trust. An apology acknowledges the impact of the actions (or inactions) that led to mistrust, while restitution seeks to make amends tangibly. This could range from refunding a dissatisfied customer to investing in community initiatives to demonstrate commitment to your values.

**Building a Culture of Accountability:** Long-term, overcoming mistrust requires more than just addressing the immediate issues; it involves creating a culture of accountability within your organization. This means establishing clear expectations for behavior and communication, implementing feedback and continuous improvement systems, and fostering an environment where honesty and integrity are valued and rewarded.

**Learning and Growing from the Experience:** Finally, overcoming mistrust is an opportunity for learning and growth. Reflecting on the causes of mistrust and the steps taken to resolve it can provide valuable insights for preventing similar issues in the future. It can also strengthen the organization by demonstrating resilience, the capacity for growth, and a commitment to maintaining strong, trust-based relationships.

In navigating the challenges of mistrust, remember that the goal is not just to return to the status quo but to emerge with more substantial, resilient, and authentic connections. This journey requires patience, commitment, and a genuine desire to act in the best interests of all stakeholders.

As we conclude this section on overcoming mistrust, we prepare to explore the correlation between trust and long-term success. Understanding this relationship is crucial for any business leader seeking to build a sustainable, growth-oriented organization founded on trust and reciprocity.

Are you ready to proceed to the next section, where we'll explore how trust is a pivotal element in ensuring sustainable business growth and success?

# Trust and Long-Term Success - Correlation between trust and sustainable business growth.

As we pivot towards the critical relationship between trust and long-term success in the business realm, it becomes evident that trust is not merely a component of business strategy but the very bedrock of sustainable growth. The linkage between trust and long-term success is profound, underscoring the notion that businesses grounded in trustful relationships are better positioned to navigate the complexities of modern markets and achieve enduring success.

**Trust as a Competitive Advantage:** Trust can be a significant differentiator for businesses in today's saturated markets. Companies that earn and maintain the trust of their customers, employees, and partners often enjoy higher loyalty levels, repeat business, and referrals. This trust translates into a competitive advantage that is difficult for competitors to replicate, setting the foundation for sustainable growth and success.

**Enhanced Stakeholder Engagement:** Trust fosters a more engaged stakeholder base. Employees who trust their employers are more committed, productive, and willing to go the extra mile. Similarly, customers who trust a company are likelier to remain loyal despite competitive offers. This heightened level of engagement contributes to a robust, resilient business capable of weathering challenges and seizing opportunities.

**Facilitating Innovation and Adaptation:** Trust within

an organization encourages a culture of innovation and adaptation. When employees trust their leaders and the company's direction, they are more likely to contribute ideas and embrace change. This culture of trust enables businesses to adapt more swiftly to market changes, embrace new technologies, and innovate, ensuring long-term relevance and success.

**Building a Strong Brand Reputation:** Trust is crucial in creating and maintaining a solid brand reputation. A trust-based reputation attracts customers, partners, and talented employees, all essential for growth. Moreover, in times of crisis, a strong trust-based reputation can mitigate negative impacts, allowing businesses to recover more quickly and maintain their trajectory toward success.

Ensuring Customer Loyalty and Retention: The correlation between trust and customer loyalty is well-documented. Customers who trust a brand are more likely to continue doing business with it and advocate for it through word-of-mouth. This loyalty is invaluable, as retaining existing customers is often more cost-effective than acquiring new ones. Trust, therefore, plays a pivotal role in ensuring customer retention and the long-term success of a business.

**Attracting Investment and Funding:** Trust is a critical factor for potential investors. Trustworthy businesses that demonstrate integrity, transparency, and a commitment to ethical practices are more likely to attract investment and funding opportunities. Investors seek out companies they believe can achieve long-term success, and trust is a vital indicator of a company's potential for sustained growth.

In conclusion, trust is not just an ethical imperative but a strategic necessity for businesses aiming for long-term success. The correlation between trust and sustainable business growth is undeniable, offering a clear path for companies willing to invest in building trustful relationships with all their stakeholders. As we have explored the importance of trust in business reciprocity, authentic connections, overcoming mistrust, and its impact on long-term success, it becomes clear that trust is the golden thread weaving through successful business practices.

As we wrap up this chapter on building trust as the foundation of reciprocity, we have explored the significance of trust in forging authentic connections, strategies to overcome mistrust, and the undeniable link between trust and sustainable growth. This exploration underscores the imperative for businesses to prioritize trust at every level of operation.

In the next and final section, we will summarize the key insights from this chapter and outline actionable steps that you, as a business leader, can take to embed these principles of trust and reciprocity within your organization. Are you ready to conclude this chapter with a focus on actionable insights and the promise of a trust-based future for your business?

## Conclusion & Action Steps

As we draw this chapter to a close, let's reflect on the transformative journey we've embarked upon together, from understanding the foundational role of trust in fostering reciprocity within the business landscape to exploring strategies for building authentic connections, overcoming mistrust, and ultimately, realizing the correlation between confidence and long-term success. Each section has been a step forward in our collective pursuit of building businesses that are not just successful in the traditional sense but are deeply rooted in trust, reciprocity, and mutual benefit.

## Action Steps to Implement Trust and Reciprocity in Your Business:

1. **Conduct a Trust Audit:** Evaluate your business practices to identify areas where trust could be strengthened. This could involve assessing customer feedback, employee satisfaction, and partner relationships to pinpoint gaps and opportunities for improvement.

2. **Develop a Plan for Authentic Engagement:** Create a comprehensive plan to enhance authentic connections with all stakeholders based on the audit findings. This could include personalized customer experiences, improved internal communication strategies, or community engagement initiatives.

3. **Implement Transparency Measures:** Make transparency a cornerstone of your business operations. This could mean more open communication channels, straightforward explanations of your business processes, and regular company performance and decision-making updates.

4. **Foster a Culture of Accountability:** Ensure that your business practices reflect the values of integrity and accountability. Encourage feedback, acknowledge mistakes, and take corrective action promptly to demonstrate your commitment to trustworthiness.

5. **Monitor and Adjust:** Trust-building is an ongoing process. Review the effectiveness of your strategies regularly and be prepared to make adjustments as necessary. Continuously seek ways to deepen trust with all stakeholders for sustained growth and success.

In embracing these action steps, remember that building a trust-based business is challenging and rewarding. It requires patience, dedication, and a genuine commitment to acting in the best interests of all stakeholders. Yet, the rewards—a loyal customer base, a motivated workforce, resilient partnerships, and sustainable growth—are immeasurable.

As we conclude this chapter, I invite you to join me in this ongoing quest to revolutionize our businesses through the power of trust and reciprocity. Together, we can create companies that thrive and communities that flourish, setting a new standard for success in the business world.

Thank you for taking this journey with me. The road ahead is bright with the promise of mutual success and shared achievements. Let's move forward with confidence, guided by the principles of trust and reciprocity, to build businesses that are not only successful but truly transformative.

As we look ahead to the next chapter, remember that each step we take is an opportunity to reinforce the values of trust and reciprocity, creating a ripple effect that extends far beyond our immediate circle. We can forge a path toward a future where business is synonymous with integrity, innovation, and mutual respect.

# 3

# Customer Loyalty through Compassionate Engagement

I N THE DYNAMIC BUSINESS landscape, where interactions are the currency of success, grasping the essence of customer loyalty emerges not as a mere advantage but as a necessity. This journey of understanding begins with embracing a fundamental truth, eloquently expressed by Maya Angelou: "People will forget what you said, forget what you did, but will never forget how you made them feel." This profound emotional connection lies at the core of genuine customer engagement.

Envision a world where every call and question is seen not just as a transaction but as an opportunity for meaningful connection. This vision isn't just aspirational; it's a reality for organizations like Apple, Nordstrom, Chick-fil-A, and the Ritz-Carlton, which stand as paragons of customer service excellence. Their success isn't merely a product of operational efficiency but a reflection of a more profound ethos that guides their interactions.

Central to this approach is the philosophy of viewing every engagement as a stepping stone towards building lasting relationships. It's about transcending the transactional framework of business and connecting on a human level. This principle became vividly clear to me through personal experiences, illustrating that even the most mundane interaction, such as a misdial, can lay the groundwork for future patronage.

I recall a poignant incident in which a caller, intending to reach a competitor, inadvertently connected with us. Rather than swiftly redirecting them, we chose to assist in locating the correct information. This act of goodwill—prioritizing their needs over immediate profit—not only won their gratitude but also inspired a decisive shift in their loyalty, favoring us over the competition.

Such experiences illuminate a crucial lesson: the enduring impact of first impressions and the transformative power of making individuals feel valued. It's about embodying a service-first mentality, showcasing our dedication to their welfare beyond commercial competition. This commitment doesn't merely attract customers; it lays the groundwork for a loyalty built on respect and mutual recognition.

Engaging customers goes beyond these initial interactions; it involves an immersive understanding of their lives, aspirations, and challenges—not as a sales tactic but as a sincere effort to elevate their experience with us. An illustrative example is simple appointment scheduling that evolved into a testament to our dedication. By genuinely understanding their context, we provided solutions that preempted discomfort, reaffirming that their satisfaction is our priority.

This customer service ethos — centered on empathetic engagement and tailored experiences — transcends traditional business strategies to become a philosophy. When adopted, it can redefine our business interactions, making every customer feel uniquely seen and valued.

In Chapter 3, we delve into "Customer Loyalty through Compassionate Engagement" and explore how to transcend transactional exchanges in favor of building genuine connections, customizing services to individual needs, and employing practical engagement strategies. This chapter serves as both a guide and a declaration for those ready to transform their approach to business through empathy and reciprocal respect.

Join us on this exploration, leveraging real-life examples and actionable insights to redefine customer service in a manner that captivates the intellect and the heart. This journey invites you to adopt a transformative business ethos, where every interaction is an avenue for fostering enduring, meaningful relationships.

## Redefining Customer Service - Moving beyond transactions to relationships.

In an era where the pace of business accelerates by the day, the reimagining of customer service has become imperative. This evolution transcends the mere exchange of goods and services, cultivating profound, enduring connections. This transformative journey isn't about adopting new tactics superficially; it's about a fundamental shift in the ethos with which businesses engage with their clientele. It's about perceiving every interaction and transaction as a golden opportunity to deepen bonds, transforming fleeting exchanges into lasting relationships.

Envision a world where businesses view their customers not as mere entries in a ledger or targets to be achieved but as co-travelers on a shared path toward growth and mutual success. This concept, far from a utopian fantasy, is a reality for organizations that have set benchmarks in customer service excellence, such as Apple, Nordstrom, Chick-fil-A, and Ritz Carlton. These entities embody the understanding that the cornerstone of sustained success rests not in the multitude of transactions processed but in the richness of the relationships nurtured.

At the heart of this relationship-centric business paradigm is the practice of active listening. This involves genuinely absorbing customers' words and grasping their needs, desires, and unarticulated expectations. Such a mindset shift demands moving from merely reacting to customer inquiries to anticipating their needs, evolving from a stance of passive service delivery to one of proactive engagement.

Personalized support emerges as a critical component in this new framework. It's about acknowledging the individuality of each customer interaction and customizing solutions to align with their specific needs and situations. This personalization could manifest in various forms, from accommodating special requests beyond the standard protocol to offering tailored product suggestions based on previous engagements or the simple act of recalling and using a customer's name during interactions. These seemingly minor acts convey a profound respect for the customer, cultivating a foundation of loyalty and trust.

Emphasizing relationships over mere transactions entails a readiness to invest time and resources into customer interactions without the immediate prospect of a sale. It's about imbuing every touchpoint with value, whether by providing expert guidance, sharing insightful content, or just offering a sympathetic ear. Such an approach transforms even the most mundane exchanges into opportunities to showcase the business's dedication to its customers, sowing the seeds for enduring loyalty.

Cultivating a customer-centric culture within the organization is equally vital. This involves educating and empowering employees across all levels to prioritize customer satisfaction, equipping them with the necessary tools and autonomy to address challenges and make impactful decisions. This culture applauds and rewards those who exceed expectations in serving customers, reinforcing the importance of relationship building.

The advantages of adopting this relationship-first approach are multifaceted. Satisfied customers are more inclined to return, make repeat purchases, and evolve into brand advocates. They are also more understanding and forgiving of occasional lapses, recognizing them as part of the business landscape. Crucially, they become ambassadors of the brand's community, proliferating their positive experiences and facilitating organic growth.

In essence, the redefinition of customer service to privilege relationships above transactions represents not merely a strategic shift but a philosophical one. It's about creating a business ecosystem that inspires love and trust, nurturing one interaction at a time. By placing a premium on the human element of business, companies can forge a loyal customer base that supports them financially and champions their mission and values. This chapter delves into actionable strategies and real-world insights, offering a blueprint for businesses aspiring to a more relationship-centric model and illustrating how to transform customer service from a function into a mission.

## Personalized Experiences - How to tailor services to individual customer needs.

Personalizing experiences emerges as a pivotal strategy in the pursuit of building lasting customer relationships. It's about crafting services and interactions that resonate personally with each customer, recognizing their unique preferences and needs. This personalization is about leveraging data and weaving empathy and understanding into every touchpoint, creating experiences that feel tailor-made and deeply relevant.

Imagine a world where businesses not only know your name but also remember your last purchase, anticipate your needs and make recommendations that feel spot on. This level of service isn't reserved for luxury brands; it's increasingly becoming the standard customers expect across all sectors. The key to unlocking this personalized world is understanding and effectively leveraging customer data. By analyzing past interactions, purchases, and preferences, businesses can create a detailed picture of each customer, allowing them to tailor their offerings to speak directly to the individual's desires.

However, personalization extends beyond just marketing messages or product recommendations. It's about the entire customer journey, from the initial contact to post-purchase support. It's about ensuring that every phone call, email, and in-person interaction is informed by a deep understanding of the customer and their value. This might mean recognizing important life events, tailoring communication styles to match customer preferences, or offering bespoke solutions to problems that consider the customer's history with the brand.

Moreover, the technology to support this level of personalization is more accessible than ever. Customer Relationship Management (CRM) systems, artificial intelligence, and big data analytics offer powerful tools for personally understanding and engaging with customers. However, more than technology is needed. The human element—empathy, understanding, and genuine connection—is irreplaceable. The combination of sophisticated technology and human insight creates genuinely personalized experiences.

Creating personalized experiences also means being proactive. It's about anticipating customer needs before they arise, offering solutions and support that surprise and delight. This proactive approach solves problems and builds trust and loyalty, showing customers that their well-being is always at the top of their minds.

Furthermore, personalization can lead to stronger customer loyalty. When customers feel seen and understood by a brand, they're more likely to continue doing business with it. They're also more likely to become advocates, sharing their positive experiences with friends and family. In this way, personalization can drive both retention and acquisition, fueling business growth.

However, personalization must be approached with care and

respect for customer privacy. Businesses must navigate the fine line between personalization and intrusion, ensuring they use customer data ethically and transparently. This means obtaining consent, providing clear value in exchange for data, and offering customers control over their information.

In conclusion, tailoring services to individual customer needs through personalized experiences is a powerful strategy for building lasting relationships. It requires a blend of technology, insight, and, most importantly, empathy. Businesses can transform transactions into meaningful interactions by focusing on the individual, fostering loyalty, and driving growth. This chapter will delve deeper into practical strategies for implementing personalization, sharing examples of businesses that have succeeded in this endeavor and offering guidance for those looking to follow in their footsteps.

## Case Studies of Loyalty - Examples of brands that have built loyal customer bases.

On the journey to cultivate enduring customer relationships, the art of personalizing experiences stands out as a cornerstone strategy. It involves creating service interactions that resonate individually, acknowledging and honoring each customer's distinct preferences and requirements. This endeavor transcends the mere utilization of data; it's about infusing every encounter with empathy and understanding, offering experiences that feel uniquely crafted and profoundly relevant to each person.

Envision a scenario where businesses not only recall your name but also remember your previous purchases, predict your future needs, and provide recommendations that astonish you with accuracy. This caliber of service, once the exclusive domain of high-end brands, is now expected in every sector. The secret to unlocking such personalized service lies in the adept harnessing of customer data. Through analyzing past interactions, purchases, and expressed preferences, organizations can paint a detailed portrait of each customer, enabling them to fine-tune their services to directly appeal to each individual's desires.

Yet, personalization encompasses more than just tailored marketing messages or product suggestions. It permeates the entire customer journey, from the first contact point to ongoing post-purchase support. It's about ensuring that every communication, whether via phone, email, or face-to-face, is enriched by a comprehensive understanding of the customer's identity and values. This could involve acknowledging significant milestones in the customer's life, adapting communication styles to suit their preferences, or crafting custom solutions to issues, considering the customer's history with the brand.

The technological infrastructure to support such intricate personalization is more accessible than ever. Tools like Customer Relationship Management (CRM) systems, artificial intelligence (AI), and big data analytics provide robust capabilities for profoundly understanding and engaging with customers personally. However, more than technology in isolation is required. The human elements—empathy, comprehension, and genuine connection—remain indispensable. The synergy of cutting-edge technology and human insight forges genuinely personalized experiences.

Embarking on personalized experiences also entails adopting a proactive stance. It's about foreseeing customer needs before they manifest, presenting solutions and support that resolve issues and engender surprise and delight. This forward-thinking approach doesn't just address problems; it cultivates trust and loyalty, reassuring customers that their well-being is always a priority.

Moreover, personalization can significantly enhance customer loyalty. When a brand recognizes and understands individuals, they are more inclined to continue their patronage. They're also more likely to become brand ambassadors, sharing exceptional experiences within their social circles. Thus, personalization is a dual engine for retention and acquisition, propelling business expansion.

Nonetheless, navigating personalization demands a careful balance, ensuring respect for customer privacy. Companies must tread the delicate line between personalization and intrusion, employing customer data ethically and transparently. This involves securing consent, delivering tangible value in exchange for data, and empowering customers with control over their information.

In sum, sculpting services to cater to each customer's unique needs through personalized experiences emerges as a potent formula for fostering deep-rooted relationships. This strategy melds technology, insight, and, paramountly, empathy. Businesses can elevate mere transactions to meaningful engagements by centering on the individual, nurturing loyalty, and stimulating growth. This section delves into actionable strategies for actualizing personalization, spotlighting businesses that have excelled in this realm, and providing a roadmap for others aspiring to emulate their success.

## Tools for Engagement - Technological and human resources that enhance customer engagement.

Navigating the intricacies of the digital age, the significance of employing a multifaceted toolkit for customer engagement cannot be overstated. This arsenal, blending the sophistication of technology with the irreplaceable value of human interaction, serves as the lifeline connecting a business's essence with its clientele. It paves the way for crafting personalized, impactful, and efficient exchanges that resonate deeply with customers, elevating the standard of relationship-building to unprecedented heights.

At the forefront of these technological marvels are Customer Relationship Management (CRM) systems, pillars for orchestrating detailed chronicles of customer engagements, preferences, and feedback. These platforms are instrumental in sculpting bespoke communication strategies and service offerings, ushering in a realm of personalization that was once relegated to the confines of imagination. Complementing these systems, marketing automation tools wield the power of targeted communications, dispatching messages and propositions that align perfectly with customers' observed behaviors and analytical profiles, thus magnifying the precision and relevance of each interaction.

Social media platforms emerge as dynamic arenas for engagement, bridging the gap between businesses and their audiences with unparalleled immediacy. These digital stages serve as conduits for swift feedback and customer support and as fertile grounds for humanizing brands, disseminating valuable content, and nurturing a sense of community. The inherently interactive nature of social media imbues it with the unique capacity to foster personal connections, engendering a loyal following through shared experiences and dialogues.

Parallel to these technological assets, the human element of customer engagement shines with equal, if not greater, significance. Customer service representatives, embodying the voice and ethos of the company, possess the transformative ability to convert potential adversities into avenues for deepening customer allegiance. Their arsenal of empathy, active listening, and adept problem-solving empowers them to meet and exceed customer expectations, delivering solutions that resonate with care and understanding.

Sales teams with exhaustive product knowledge and a keen sense of customer aspirations play a pivotal role in tailoring recommendations that enhance the customer journey. The commitment to continuous learning and skill enhancement for these teams ensures they can engage customers in discussions that are informative and deeply relevant to the customer's unique context.

Weaving these technological and human elements into a coherent engagement strategy demands a profound comprehension of the available tools and the nuanced art of human connection. This blend of technology and personal touch is not just about engaging customers more effectively; it's about forging enduring bonds anchored in trust, satisfaction, and mutual respect. By adeptly harnessing these resources, businesses can transcend traditional transactional dynamics, cultivating relationships rich in loyalty and advocacy, thus propelling themselves towards sustained growth and success in the fiercely competitive business landscape.

In essence, the symbiosis of cutting-edge technology and human insight forms the cornerstone for businesses aspiring to elevate customer engagement and loyalty. These instruments, when wielded with skill and sensitivity, have the potential to metamorphose routine customer interactions into memorable encounters that not only satisfy but also inspire. This comprehensive approach to customer engagement, embracing both the precision of technology and the warmth of human connection, lays the groundwork for a thriving enterprise that cherishes and nurtures its most valuable asset: its customers.

## Conclusion and Action Steps

As we conclude this exploration of "Customer Loyalty through Compassionate Engagement," it's clear that cultivating deep, meaningful customer relationships is both a strategic imperative and a transformative opportunity for businesses. This chapter has underscored the essence of moving beyond transactional interactions to creating personalized experiences that resonate deeply with customers, fostering a sense of loyalty that transcends the ordinary.

Businesses can unlock unparalleled growth and sustainability by redefining customer service to prioritize relationships, tailoring services to individual needs, learning from case studies of brands that excel in loyalty, and leveraging both technological and human resources for engagement. These strategies not only enhance customer satisfaction but also drive advocacy, turning customers into brand champions.

To implement these insights, here are five actionable steps:

1. Invest in CRM and marketing automation tools to better understand and anticipate customer needs.

2. Train your team in empathy and active listening, emphasizing the importance of every customer interaction.

3. Personalize the customer experience at every touchpoint, from marketing to sales to customer service.

4. Gather and act on customer feedback to continuously improve and adapt your offerings.

5. Create a customer-centric culture within your organization where every employee understands and contributes to the customer loyalty mission.

Embracing these strategies requires a commitment to continuous improvement and an unwavering focus on the customer. The journey toward building a business that thrives on compassionate engagement and reciprocal value is challenging but immensely rewarding. It's a path that leads to economic success and creating a brand loved, respected, and advocated for by those it serves.

Remember the power of making customers feel valued and understood when embarking on this journey. This is the key to unlocking a world of possibilities where business growth and customer satisfaction go hand in hand, fostering a cycle of success that benefits all.

# 4

# Cultivating a Positive Workplace Through Reciprocity

I N MY JOURNEY AS a leader, I've discovered the transformative power of reciprocity in the workplace. It's a principle that, when embedded into an organization's core values, can revolutionize how teams interact, collaborate, and perform. My experience has shown me that our customers need to feel cared for, and so too do our employees. The essence of this realization came to life through a series of initiatives to foster a culture of give-and-take within my team.

Drawing inspiration from "Drive: The Surprising Truth About What Motivates Us" by Daniel H. Pink, I embarked on a mission to transform a demotivated team into a highly productive unit. Pink's insights into motivation resonated deeply, illuminating the path forward. It wasn't about financial incentives alone but about fulfilling deeper human needs: autonomy, mastery, and purpose. This understanding laid the groundwork for the changes I aimed to implement.

The challenge was clear: how could I instill a sense of purpose and mutual respect in a team that had hit a plateau? The answer lies in the concept of reciprocity. By integrating this into our daily operations, I aimed to show my team the level of dedication and customer service I expected, thereby driving positive results in their performance and overall experience.

One of my first initiatives was to launch outreach campaigns, allowing the team to choose causes they felt passionate about. This approach empowered them and aligned with our broader mission of serving beyond our immediate business interests. When one team struggled to identify a cause, I stepped in with suggestions, ultimately deciding on a toy donation drive for a local children's hospital.

The results were nothing short of remarkable. The campaign boosted customer engagement and significantly increased our revenue, marking September as the highest-grossing month in our company's history. But more importantly, it instilled a sense of pride and motivation within the team. Witnessing the joy our efforts brought to the children and seeing the positive feedback from the community reinforced the value of our work beyond the bottom line.

This experience underscored the profound impact of reciprocity on employee engagement. By showing our team that we valued their contributions and cared about their well-being, we cultivated an environment where motivation flourished. The shift towards remote work, highlighted by recent global events, has only reinforced the importance of maintaining and enhancing these connections. Despite the physical distance, the principles of reciprocity remain a powerful tool for fostering a positive and productive workplace culture.

Statistics support this approach, with companies boasting highly engaged workforces outperforming their peers significantly. This data validates the strategies we've implemented and serves as a compelling argument for the power of a motivated team.

As we delve deeper into this chapter, I'll share more about the role of reciprocity in employee motivation, practical steps for implementing reciprocal practices, case studies of successful companies, and tools for measuring the impact. My hope is that by sharing my journey, I can inspire other leaders to embrace the principles of reciprocity and create workplaces that thrive on mutual respect, engagement, and shared success.

## The Role of Reciprocity in Employee Motivation - Understanding the Connection.

Embarking on a journey to uncover the intricate link between reciprocity and employee motivation has fundamentally reshaped my leadership approach. This epiphany struck me during a tumultuous phase when the spirit of my team had noticeably dwindled. Despite being a collective of highly skilled individuals, there was a palpable absence of zeal and ambition. In this critical moment, I pivoted towards the tenets of reciprocity, integrating them into our foundational principles, and observed an extraordinary evolution.

Reciprocity, defined as the mutual exchange of advantages or favors, became our beacon of hope. My initial steps involved sincerely recognizing my team's diligence, both in private and public forums, and offering genuine significant rewards. This approach wasn't rooted in lavish displays but in a heartfelt acknowledgment of each person's contribution and its ripple effect on our unified success.

This transformation unfolded slowly but unmistakably. A palpable shift in the work environment emerged when I dedicated effort to grasping and nurturing my team's professional goals and personal well-being. Team members felt acknowledged and esteemed, not merely as employees but as vital components of the organization's essence. This newfound appreciation and respect elicited a mutual reaction; they commenced taking enhanced responsibility for their tasks, fostering improved collaboration, and extending support to one another beyond my initial expectations.

Our path to nurturing a positive workplace through reciprocity also entailed reimagining our response to obstacles and failures. Rather than resorting to blame or criticism, we emphasized collective problem-solving, learning from our missteps, and jointly celebrating our achievements. This approach cultivated a culture steeped in trust and mutual respect, where open feedback was encouraged, and every individual's perspective was valued.

The principle of reciprocity transcended the boundaries of our team, affecting our interactions with other departments and our clientele. We adopted a more open and generous stance, eagerly sharing our insights and resources and committed to our shared success. This not only bolstered our team's morale and efficiency but also had a tangible positive effect on customer satisfaction and the growth of our business.

Upon reflecting on this transformative journey, I've recognized that the core of team motivation lies not in tangible rewards but in the depth and quality of the relationships we forge. It's about cultivating an ecosystem where reciprocity thrives, where each member feels acknowledged and driven to offer their utmost. This detailed exploration delves into the significance of reciprocity in enhancing employee motivation, offering actionable insights and strategies for leaders eager to develop a positive and high-performing workplace culture.

Through this narrative, we'll examine the practical applications of reciprocity, from personalized acknowledgments to fostering a supportive environment that values individual and collective growth. Leaders will learn how to implement these principles to elevate team morale and drive sustainable business success. This chapter aims to equip you with the knowledge and tools to transform your leadership style, ensuring your team feels truly valued and motivated to achieve greatness, embodying the essence of "Profit with Purpose."

## Implementing Reciprocal Practices - Practical steps to encourage a give-and-take culture.

Integrating reciprocal practices within my organization embarked us on a transformative path, demanding meticulous planning, transparent communication, and a steadfast dedication to nurturing a culture rooted in mutual exchange and support. This evolution was not just about recognizing efforts; it was fundamentally about establishing a culture where every individual felt valued and empowered to contribute, share insights, and pursue growth.

The journey commenced with fostering open dialogue and collaboration across the organizational hierarchy. I spearheaded the initiation of consistent team gatherings, ensuring a platform where voices could be heard, ideas exchanged, concerns aired, and feedback shared freely. These meetings transcended routine project discussions, evolving into forums for celebrating achievements, identifying learning moments, and collaboratively brainstorming solutions. Such practices were instrumental in dismantling barriers and cultivating a community ethos imbued with a shared mission.

A pivotal element in this cultural shift was the acknowledgment and celebration of generosity and teamwork. I introduced a system where peers could commend colleagues for their exceptional support or contributions toward our collective objectives. These accolades were shared publicly, reinforcing the significance we place on collaboration and mutual aid within our organization.

To deepen the roots of reciprocal practices, I was keen on creating avenues for professional enrichment and personal development. This encompassed mentoring schemes, knowledge exchange sessions, and opportunities for cross-functional training. The intent was to foster an environment where growth and learning were inherently reciprocal activities, with each member both a mentor and a learner, enriching and being enriched in turn.

Equity and clarity in decision-making were equally paramount. I endeavored to involve team members in pivotal decisions, ensuring a variety of perspectives were considered, thereby not only enriching the decision-making process but also fostering a culture of ownership and responsibility among the team.

The integration of these reciprocal measures heralded a significant transformation in our organizational culture. We observed a marked increase in engagement, motivation, and a collective commitment to our goals. The emergence of a strong sense of belonging and mutual respect contributed to enhanced productivity, innovation, and overall job fulfillment among team members.

This journey underscored that the implementation of reciprocal practices is a marathon, not a sprint, necessitating patience, resilience, and a deep-seated commitment to cultivating a supportive and positive workplace. It revolves around leading by example, demonstrating empathy, and appreciating the distinct contributions of each team member. As I forge ahead in leading my organization, my resolve to promote a culture of reciprocity remains unwavering, driven by a vision where every individual feels appreciated, supported, and inspired to excel.

This not only charts the course of integrating reciprocity into the fabric of organizational culture but also serves as a testament to the transformative power of mutual respect and support. It's a journey of learning, adaptation, and commitment to principles that foster a thriving, dynamic, and inclusive workplace where reciprocity acts as the cornerstone for sustainable success and collective achievement.

## Case Studies - Companies that have successfully enhanced employee morale through reciprocity.

Diving deep into the essence of reciprocity and its monumental role in fostering a vibrant workplace culture, I find myself drawn to the compelling narratives of organizations that have masterfully leveraged this principle. These tales are not just stories; they are beacons of inspiration, showcasing the profound ways in which embedding reciprocal values can dramatically uplift employee morale, boost productivity, and elevate overall company performance. Allow me to share these insights, drawing from my own journey and the pioneering strategies of industry giants.

At the heart of Google's success lies an inventive approach to employee engagement that exemplifies the essence of reciprocity in action. Google champions the autonomy and creative freedom of its employees by dedicating 20% of their time to pursue projects that spark their personal interest. This innovative policy does more than just encourage creativity; it embodies a deep-seated respect for employees' aspirations, fostering a nurturing environment for professional growth. The resultant innovation and loyalty among Google's workforce are a testament to the mutual benefits derived from this reciprocal respect. Witnessing Google's achievements, I am reminded of the importance of nurturing an environment where employees feel valued and inspired to explore their passions.

Similarly, Southwest Airlines' narrative is a powerful testament to the value of reciprocal trust and empowerment within a company. By encouraging employees to take full ownership of customer experiences, Southwest has cultivated a culture brimming with mutual trust and respect. This empowerment translates into a workforce that is deeply engaged, taking pride in their contributions and going above and beyond to ensure customer satisfaction. The airline's outstanding customer service and robust financial health can be directly attributed to this culture of employee empowerment. Reflecting on Southwest's approach, I see the undeniable impact of fostering an environment where employees feel trusted and valued, motivating them to contribute their best.

Zappos stands out for its unwavering commitment to employee happiness and well-being, fostering a workplace culture that prioritizes mutual support and appreciation. Through peer-to-peer recognition programs and a focus on work-life harmony, Zappos has crafted an environment where employee satisfaction is paramount. This culture of mutual care and recognition has propelled Zappos to remarkable heights in customer satisfaction and loyalty, underscoring the reciprocal relationship between employee well-being and company success. As I ponder Zappos' strategy, I am inspired by the power of a supportive and appreciative workplace that drives both employee fulfillment and business achievements.

These illustrious companies—Google, Southwest Airlines, and Zappos—serve as shining examples of the transformative potential of reciprocity in the workplace. Their success stories illuminate the path for leaders seeking to cultivate a thriving environment, highlighting the undeniable link between investing in employees and achieving business excellence. As I assimilate the lessons from these pioneers, I am invigorated by the prospect of championing reciprocal practices within my own organization. The journey towards cultivating a culture where every team member feels genuinely valued and empowered is both challenging and rewarding.

In embracing the principles of reciprocity, the objective is clear: to create a workspace where mutual respect, trust, and support are the foundations upon which productivity and innovation flourish. These case studies not only reinforce my belief in the power of reciprocity but also serve as a blueprint for instilling similar values in my own corporate ethos. By prioritizing the well-being, growth, and satisfaction of employees, the potential for fostering a dynamic, motivated, and highly productive workforce is immense.

As I continue to navigate the complexities of leadership, the stories of Google, Southwest Airlines, and Zappos stand as guiding stars, illuminating the path toward achieving a workplace that thrives on the principles of mutual benefit and respect. The journey of embedding reciprocal practices is ongoing, a constant evolution towards creating an environment where every individual feels empowered to contribute their best and secure in the knowledge that their well-being and aspirations are valued. This commitment to fostering a reciprocal culture is not just a strategy for enhancing employee morale and productivity; it is a testament to the belief that the success of an organization is inextricably linked to the happiness and engagement of its workforce.

## Measuring the Impact - Tools and methods to gauge employee engagement and motivation.

Measuring the impact of employee engagement and motivation within my organization has been a critical part of our journey toward creating a workplace culture rooted in the principles of reciprocity. Recognizing the value and effectiveness of our initiatives in fostering a supportive and positive environment required a multifaceted approach, combining both qualitative and quantitative methods to capture a holistic view of our progress.

Our strategy for gauging employee engagement started with the deployment of comprehensive anonymous surveys. These instruments were meticulously designed to elicit honest feedback on various aspects of the workplace experience, from job satisfaction and personal growth opportunities to the effectiveness of management and the sense of belonging within the team. The insights garnered from these surveys were instrumental in identifying both strengths to build upon and areas in need of attention.

Beyond surveys, we established robust feedback mechanisms to encourage ongoing dialogue between employees and leadership. Regular one-on-one meetings, an open-door policy, and feedback sessions were instituted as platforms for open communication. These interactions served not only as a means to address immediate concerns but also to foster a culture of transparency and trust. They provided rich qualitative data that complemented the survey findings, offering more profound insights into the dynamics of our team's engagement and motivation.

Performance evaluations and the monitoring of key performance indicators (KPIs) were other critical components of our strategy. By setting clear, achievable goals and regularly reviewing progress, we could not only measure productivity and efficiency but also identify opportunities for professional development. This approach helped recognize and celebrate achievements, thereby reinforcing a positive feedback loop that motivated employees to maintain high performance levels.

In implementing these measures, we also paid close attention to the nuances of collecting and interpreting data. We ensured that our methods respected privacy and confidentiality, thereby encouraging candidness in responses. Moreover, we adopted a continuous improvement mindset, using the data collected to refine our strategies and initiatives in real time. This iterative process allowed us to adapt quickly to changing needs and to sustain our culture of reciprocity effectively.

Reflecting on the impact of these measures, it's evident that they have significantly contributed to enhancing our workplace environment. The insights gained have enabled us to implement targeted interventions designed to boost morale, improve job satisfaction, and increase overall engagement. These efforts have not only led to tangible improvements in team cohesion and productivity but have also reinforced our commitment to creating a workplace where every employee feels valued, heard, and motivated.

As I look to the future, I'm committed to continuing this journey of fostering a workplace culture that thrives on mutual respect, support, and reciprocity. By maintaining our focus on measuring and enhancing employee engagement and motivation, we can ensure a dynamic and thriving work environment. This commitment to continuous improvement and responsiveness to our team's needs will remain central to our efforts as we strive to achieve not just organizational success but also personal fulfillment and growth for every member of our team.

In closing, the journey of embedding reciprocity into our organizational culture has taught me the invaluable lesson that the strength of our team lies in our collective commitment to each other's success. By prioritizing the well-being and engagement of our employees, we pave the way for not just individual achievement but for the sustained success of our entire organization. This chapter, though merely a snapshot of our ongoing journey, encapsulates the essence of our approach and the profound impact it has had on our workplace. It stands as a testament to the power of reciprocity in transforming not just business outcomes but the very lives of those we work alongside every day.

## Conclusion and Action Steps

As I reflect on the journey of integrating reciprocity into the very fabric of our workplace, the transformation has been profound. This chapter, woven with personal insights, strategies, and examples, aims not just to narrate a success story but to offer a blueprint for cultivating a positive, motivated workplace grounded in the principles of mutual respect and support.

The journey began with a realization of the transformative power of reciprocity—a principle that, when embraced, has the potential to elevate not just individual performance but the collective spirit of an organization. Implementing reciprocal practices required a thoughtful blend of strategic initiatives and a genuine commitment to fostering an environment where every team member feels valued and empowered.

The cornerstone of our success lies in the steps we took to measure and understand the impact of these initiatives. Through engagement surveys, feedback mechanisms, and performance evaluations, we gained invaluable insights that guided our journey. These tools not only provide a snapshot of our progress but also illuminated the path forward, enabling us to continuously refine our approach and deepen our commitment to our team's well-being and motivation.

In conclusion, cultivating a positive workplace through reciprocity is an ongoing journey. It demands persistence, empathy, and a genuine commitment to creating an environment where everyone feels supported and valued. As leaders, our role is to champion this culture, leading by example and continuously seeking ways to enrich our team's experience.

## Action Steps:

1. **Continue Open Communication:** Regularly engage in open dialogues with your team, encouraging feedback and sharing successes and challenges alike.

2. **Recognize and Reward:** Maintain a culture of recognition by celebrating acts of generosity, collaboration, and excellence.

3. **Foster Professional Growth:** Create opportunities for learning and development, encouraging skill-sharing and mentorship.

4. **Measure and Adapt:** Utilize engagement surveys and performance data to gauge the effectiveness of your initiatives, always looking for ways to improve.

5. **Lead by Example:** Embody the principles of reciprocity in your leadership style, demonstrating the values you wish to see in your team.

As we move forward, let's carry the lessons learned and the successes achieved into our ongoing efforts to create a workplace where reciprocity, respect, and mutual support are at the heart of everything we do.

# 5

# Enhancing Brand Image Through Generosity

As I REFLECT ON my journey through various careers, from managing a network of dental offices to engaging in initiatives that resonate with community and compassion, I've come to understand the profound impact of generosity on brand image. This understanding is not just theoretical but grounded in personal experience and the realization that the essence of a truly impactful brand extends far beyond the confines of its products or services. It's about how a brand integrates into the fabric of society and how it uplifts and contributes, transforming transactions into meaningful relationships. This chapter, "Enhancing Brand Image Through Generosity," is a testament to that belief and a guide to embedding generosity into the very DNA of a brand.

My journey into the heart of corporate generosity began in an unexpected setting—a network of 25 dental offices, where the opportunity to turn professional expertise into a beacon of hope for those in need presented itself. Here, I championed an initiative not just to offer dental care but to weave a narrative of compassion and community engagement that would redefine our brand's image.

The initiative was simple yet ambitious. We aimed to provide free dental care to those unable to afford treatment, tapping into our client base and community networks for nominations. This endeavor required the logistical orchestration of coordinating with shelters and rallying the dental teams for a day of volunteerism and a deep commitment to the principle of reciprocity. The response was overwhelming—200 nominations poured in, and on a crisp Saturday in February, we served 198 patients, offering treatments that amounted to $158,000 in free dental care.

This act of generosity did not go unnoticed. The reverberations of our efforts echoed through the communities we served, transforming public perception and solidifying our image as a brand that genuinely cares. The following year, 24 out of the 25 offices reported the highest net revenue in company history—a testament to the power of generosity in fostering brand loyalty and community support.

But why does generosity hold such transformative power for a brand? At its core, generosity is a universal language, a currency of goodwill that transcends cultural and economic barriers. It embodies the famous quote by Winston Churchill, "We make a living by what we get, but we make a life by what we give." This philosophy is the cornerstone of ethical branding, where actions speak louder than words, and the impact of a brand is measured not just in profit margins but in the positive changes it brings to society.

Ethical branding, therefore, is not a mere marketing strategy but a comprehensive approach to business that prioritizes transparency, social responsibility, and sustainability. It's about aligning a brand's operations and objectives with the broader values and concerns of its customers and the community. In today's digital age, where information is readily accessible, and consumer awareness is high, the ethical brand stands out. It attracts customers looking for products or services that align with their values and employees, investors, and partners who share a common vision for a better world.

The importance of ethics in modern branding cannot be overstated. Consumers increasingly make conscious choices, opting for brands committed to fair labor practices, environmental sustainability, and active community engagement. These considerations are no longer optional but essential for brands looking to establish a positive image and foster long-term relationships with their stakeholders.

By prioritizing ethical considerations, a brand differentiates itself in a crowded market and builds a foundation of trust and loyalty with its customers. This trust is invaluable, catalyzing genuine connections and engagements that go beyond the superficial. Moreover, ethical branding resonates deeply with employees and other stakeholders, creating a ripple effect that amplifies the brand's positive impact. It fosters a culture of integrity and accountability, where everyone associated with the brand is motivated by a shared purpose to do good.

In essence, enhancing a brand's image through generosity is

both a strategic and moral undertaking. It requires a deep understanding of the values that drive consumer behavior and a commitment to embedding them into every aspect of the brand's operations. This approach ensures the brand's relevance and resilience in a rapidly changing world and positions it as a leader in the movement towards a more ethical, sustainable, and compassionate marketplace.

As we delve deeper into this chapter, we will explore the practical aspects of ethical branding, from implementing acts of generosity to understanding their far-reaching impacts. Through personal stories, case studies, and a detailed analysis of the ethical brand, we aim to provide a comprehensive guide for businesses looking to make a meaningful difference in the world while enhancing their brand image. This is not just a chapter on marketing strategies; it's a call to action for brands to embrace their potential as agents of positive change, leveraging generosity to build lasting relationships and a legacy of goodwill.

## The Ethical Brand - The importance of ethics in modern branding.

In my journey through the diverse landscapes of business, from the bustling corridors of dental offices to the innovative frontiers of various industries, I've recognized the profound significance of ethics in modern branding. Much like a lighthouse guiding ships through tumultuous seas, this revelation illuminated the path for the organizations I've had the privilege to lead, steering us towards practices that resonate deeply with the core values of our customers and broader communities.

I've learned that ethical branding is not merely a facet of business strategy; it's the very bedrock upon which lasting relationships with consumers are built. It encompasses a commitment to transparency, social responsibility, and sustainable practices that go beyond the conventional metrics of success. In an era where consumers are increasingly vigilant about the integrity of the brands they support, prioritizing ethics has become indispensable.

Through my experiences, especially the transformative project with the dental offices, I've witnessed firsthand how ethical considerations can forge a powerful connection with consumers. We embarked on a journey to provide top-notch dental care and do so with a conscience. Our commitment to fairness, environmental sustainability, and community engagement became the pillars of our brand, distinguishing us in a competitive market.

Our approach to ethical branding was multifaceted. It involved rigorous transparency in our operations, ensuring our patients and their families understood the values guiding our practices. We also embraced social responsibility with open arms, engaging in initiatives that reached out to the underprivileged in our community, offering them free dental care they would otherwise be unable to afford. This uplifted the recipients and galvanized our team, imbuing them with a sense of purpose and pride in their work.

Sustainability was another cornerstone of our ethos. We meticulously integrated eco-friendly practices into our operations, from reducing office waste to adopting green technologies. This resonated with our environmentally conscious customers, reinforcing their trust in us as a brand that cares not only for their health but also for the planet.

The ripple effects of these ethical practices were profound. Not only did they enhance our brand's image in the eyes of our customers, but they also fostered a culture of integrity and accountability within our organization. Our employees, from receptionists to dental surgeons, felt part of a noble endeavor that transcended the daily routines of dental care to touch lives and make a tangible difference in the world.

Moreover, our ethical stance attracted conscientious consumers who diligently seek out brands that align with their values. These individuals became our patients and advocates, spreading the word about our work and ethos through their networks. This organic advocacy bolstered our brand's visibility and credibility, leading to sustained growth and success.

Reflecting on this chapter of my career, it's clear that ethical branding is not a mere trend but a fundamental shift in how businesses operate and engage with their audiences. It challenges us to look beyond profit margins and market share and consider the broader impact of our actions on society and the environment. It beckons us to build brands that thrive economically and contribute positively to the world.

This journey towards becoming an ethical brand has been both challenging and rewarding. It required us to rethink our priorities, to innovate and adapt our practices, and to lead with empathy and compassion. But the rewards have been immeasurable. We've built lasting relationships with our customers, fostered loyalty among our employees, and set a precedent for being a responsible business in the 21st century.

As I share these insights and experiences, I hope to inspire other businesses to embark on their own journeys of ethical branding. The path is not always easy, but the destination—a brand that stands as a beacon of integrity, responsibility, and generosity—is undoubtedly worth the effort. Let us strive to make a living not just by what we get but by what we give, embodying the timeless wisdom of Winston Churchill and transforming our businesses into forces for good in the world.

## Acts of Generosity - Simple yet effective ways to demonstrate corporate generosity.

Embarking on the path of corporate generosity, I've discovered, is an exploration of the heart and soul of a business. Reflecting upon my diverse career trajectory, which notably included stewardship of 25 dental offices, generosity became a beacon that illuminated our community outreach and defined our brand's identity. This realization dawned on me during a pivotal meeting with the organization's leaders, where I championed the cause of engaging our community through acts of reciprocity. Drawing from a reservoir of past experiences, I proposed an initiative that would address an immediate need and forge a deeper connection with our clientele and the community at large.

The initiative was simple in concept yet profound in impact: a day of free dentistry to those in dire need, identified through stories shared by our clients and team members and in collaboration with a local homeless shelter. This was not just about offering dental services; it was about acknowledging the humanity behind each patient and recognizing the broader role we could play in their lives. The enthusiasm with which this proposal was met by the dental teams was heartening, to say the least. Together, we compiled a list of 200 patients, culminating in a day where 198 individuals received critical dental care, amounting to $158,000 of free dentistry. The ripple effect of this generosity was monumental, not only in the word-of-mouth acclaim it generated but also in the tangible uplift in net revenue across nearly all offices. This initiative became a cornerstone of our annual operations, a testament to the enduring power of generosity.

Drawing from this profound experience, corporate generosity need not be a grandiose gesture; instead, it's the simple, heartfelt actions that resonate most deeply. One such gesture is encouraging employees to volunteer their time and expertise to local charities or community projects. This not only aids those in need but also instills a sense of purpose and pride within the company fabric. Supporting local businesses and suppliers, offering pro bono services or discounts to non-profit organizations, and implementing sustainable practices that benefit the environment are all facets of corporate generosity. No matter its scale, each act contributes to a tapestry of positivity and goodwill that extends far beyond the company's immediate sphere.

This approach to generosity is not merely about altruism; it's a strategic pivot towards creating a brand that is as compassionate as competent. By weaving acts of generosity into the fabric of our operations, we elevate our brand and inspire a movement within the industry. It's a testament to the belief that businesses have the power and responsibility to effect positive change in the world.

Moreover, these acts of generosity serve as a beacon for attracting like-minded individuals—both customers and employees—who share a vision for a better world. They are the building blocks for a community that values kindness, compassion, and reciprocity, which are increasingly becoming the hallmarks of successful brands in today's conscious market.

In reflecting on the journey of incorporating generosity into our business model, I am reminded of the countless ways these acts have enhanced our brand image and enriched our lives. The smiles of gratitude, the stories of relief, and the community's embrace are the true measures of success. They remind us that at the heart of every business are people—people who yearn for connection, understanding, and kindness.

As we move forward, let this chapter serve as both a reflection and a roadmap for businesses aspiring to cultivate a culture of generosity. The path is lined with opportunities to make a difference, touch lives, and reimagine what success means. It's a journey that requires courage, conviction, and, above all, a generous heart.

In sum, giving back is not just a facet of corporate responsibility; it's the essence of a brand that aspires to make a meaningful impact globally. It's a testament to the power of generosity to transform not just the recipients' lives but also the giver's soul. As we continue to navigate the complexities of the business world, let us carry with us the enduring truth that our most significant legacy is not what we accumulate but what we contribute.

## The Ripple Effect - How small acts can lead to big changes in brand perception.

In my ventures across various sectors, from the bustling world of dental care to the broader realms of business, I've come to understand the profound impact of small acts of kindness and generosity. This understanding is not just theoretical; it's deeply personal, rooted in my experiences and observations of how seemingly minor gestures can create waves of positive change.

The concept of the ripple effect, the idea that small acts can lead to significant shifts in brand perception, resonated deeply with me. It's akin to the gentle dropping of a pebble into a still pond; the ripples extend far beyond the initial point of contact, touching distant shores. In business, every interaction, no matter how small, carries with it the potential to significantly alter the perception of a brand. This principle became a guiding light in our operations, particularly during the initiative to provide free dental care to those in need.

This initiative, though specific in its aim, served as a microcosm of the broader impact small gestures can have. By offering a day of free dentistry, we were not just addressing immediate health concerns; we were signaling a more profound commitment to the well-being of our community. This commitment, rooted in genuine care and empathy, reverberated throughout the community, enhancing our brand's image as a compassionate and trustworthy partner.

Consistently delivering exceptional customer service, going the extra mile for clients, and demonstrating genuine care in every interaction became our brand's hallmark. Though simple in execution, these practices were profound in their impact. They built a foundation of trust and reliability that attracted and retained customers, turning them into vocal advocates for our brand.

Moreover, responding promptly and effectively to customer feedback and concerns underscored our commitment to continuous improvement and excellence. This responsiveness, a small act, was influential in shaping the brand's reputation. It conveyed that we valued our customers' input and were dedicated to meeting and exceeding their expectations.

The cumulative effect of these small acts was transformative. Over time, they shaped the overall perception of our brand, contributing to a narrative of reliability, empathy, and excellence. In today's interconnected world, where experiences are shared rapidly across social media and review platforms, the impact of these small acts is amplified, reaching an audience far beyond our immediate customer base.

This realization underscored the importance of nurturing every customer interaction with care, respect, and authenticity. It highlighted that in the grand tapestry of a brand's story, every thread, no matter how seemingly insignificant, plays a crucial role in defining its character and legacy.

Reflecting on this journey, I am continually inspired by the potential of small acts to initiate significant change. This principle has guided our customer service practices and become a cornerstone of our brand ethos. It's a reminder that the smallest gesture of kindness or service can be the most powerful in the pursuit of excellence.

As we move forward, let this chapter serve as a testament to the transformative power of the ripple effect in business. It's a call to action for brands to recognize the value of every interaction and approach each to create positive, lasting impressions. In doing so, we enhance our brand's image and contribute to a culture of kindness, respect, and mutual growth.

In conclusion, the journey of integrating small acts of generosity into our business practices has been both enlightening and profoundly rewarding. It has taught us that the essence of a successful brand lies not just in the quality of its products or services but in the depth of its relationships with customers and the community. By embracing this principle, we can build brands that are successful in the traditional sense and revered for their character, compassion, and contribution to the greater good.

## Case Studies - Brands that have successfully improved their image through ethical practices.

My journey through business has been marked by a series of enlightening encounters and initiatives, each contributing to a mosaic of experiences that underscore the value of ethical practices. Among these, the initiative to provide free dental care is a testament to the transformative power of moral actions for the recipients and the brand itself. This chapter of my career has illuminated the broader implications of such practices, highlighting how they can serve as beacons for brands seeking to navigate the complex waters of modern consumer expectations.

Drawing from this wellspring of experiences, I've had the privilege to witness firsthand the impact of brands that have successfully woven ethical practices into the very fabric of their identity. Companies like Patagonia and TOMS have emerged as exemplars in this regard, their stories not just narratives of business success but parables of the profound relationship between ethical conduct and brand image.

Patagonia, with its unwavering commitment to environmental sustainability, has always been a source of inspiration for me. Their approach to business, which places the planet and its well-being at the core of every decision, has set a new standard for sustainability and cultivated a fiercely loyal customer base. This alignment of values between brand and consumer has fostered a deep trust and admiration, elevating Patagonia from a mere outdoor apparel provider to a symbol of environmental stewardship. Their initiatives, from using recycled materials to advocating for the preservation of natural landscapes, resonate with a growing segment of consumers who seek to support businesses that reflect their concerns for the planet.

Similarly, TOMS' pioneering "One for One" model, where shoes are donated for every pair sold, has profoundly influenced my understanding of corporate generosity. This simple yet powerful idea has demonstrated how businesses can serve as engines for positive change, addressing global challenges through innovative business models. TOMS has sold shoes and a vision of a better world, engaging consumers not just as customers but as partners in a shared mission. The brand's ability to connect its commercial success with tangible social impact has fostered a positive brand perception that transcends the traditional product quality or price metrics.

These case studies, among others, have served as guiding stars in my own quest to blend ethical practices with business strategy. They underscore the reality that today's consumers are not just passive purchasers but active participants in a global ecosystem, eager to support brands that demonstrate a commitment to principles that extend beyond profit.

Reflecting on the impact of our free dentistry day, I see parallels with the journeys of Patagonia and TOMS. Our initiative, though modest in comparison, shared a common thread with these giants—the belief that business can and should be a force for good. The overwhelming response from the community and the subsequent success of our dental offices reinforced my conviction that ethical practices, particularly those rooted in generosity and compassion, are not just morally right but also strategically sound.

Incorporating ethical practices into a brand's DNA is not a mere marketing strategy; it's a fundamental reimagining of the business's role in society. It's about recognizing that every product sold and every service rendered is part of a larger narrative—one that encompasses the well-being of our communities, the health of our planet, and the legacy we wish to leave for future generations.

As I share these insights, I hope to inspire others to embark on their own journeys of ethical branding. The path comes with its challenges, requiring us to confront difficult questions about the nature of our businesses and the impact of our decisions. Yet, the rewards are immeasurable, offering a vision of success that is not just measured financially but in the positive changes we bring to the world.

In conclusion, my experiences have taught me that at the intersection of ethics and business lies the potential for brands to thrive and lead with purpose, integrity, and compassion. By looking at the examples of brands like Patagonia and TOMS and reflecting on our own initiatives, we can begin to chart a course towards a future where business is synonymous with benevolence, and success is measured not just by what we achieve but by what we contribute.

## Conclusion and Action Steps

Continuing on this path of ethical practice and corporate generosity, my personal journey and the initiatives I've spearheaded have deeply intertwined with the broader narrative of brands making significant strides through their commitment to doing good. Reflecting on these endeavors, I'm drawn to further elaborate on the case studies of Patagonia and TOMS, as they embody the essence of leveraging business as a platform for positive change.

My experiences, particularly the initiative to provide comprehensive dental care to those in need, resonate with the ethos these brands represent. Though distinct in its field, this venture shared the universal principles of empathy, responsibility, and community engagement that these iconic brands have championed. Through this initiative, I witnessed the tangible impact of ethical practices on brand perception and loyalty. The community's gratitude and the heightened morale within our team underscored a fundamental truth: acts of generosity and commitment to ethical practices do not just enhance a brand's image; they redefine its purpose and place in society.

Patagonia's relentless pursuit of environmental sustainability has set it apart as a leader in ethical business practices and forged a deep connection with its customers. This connection transcends the conventional buyer-seller relationship, creating a community united by shared values and a common vision for the future. My admiration for Patagonia stems from its ability to inspire action beyond its immediate sphere, influencing individuals and businesses to reconsider their environmental impact. Their initiatives, from donating a portion of sales to environmental causes to encouraging the repair and reuse of their products, exemplify how businesses can effectively balance profitability with planetary stewardship.

Similarly, TOMS' innovative "One for One" model illuminated the potential of integrating philanthropy with business. This approach, pioneering in its simplicity and impact, demonstrated how the act of purchasing could be transformed into an act of giving. What struck me most profoundly was the ripple effect of such a model—how it addressed immediate needs and sparked a broader movement towards socially responsible consumerism. TOMS has shown that ethical practices can be a powerful catalyst for brand loyalty, transforming customers into advocates for the brand's mission.

I see a shared transformation narrative that parallels these case studies and our dental care initiative. Each story is a testament to the power of brands to effect real change, challenge the status quo, and inspire a collective shift toward greater social responsibility. These brands and our own efforts underscore the reality that ethical practices are not peripheral to business success but central to it. They are the means through which a brand can truly resonate with its audience, build lasting relationships, and carve out a distinctive identity in a crowded marketplace.

This journey of integrating ethical practices into the fabric of a brand is both challenging and rewarding. It demands a willingness to look beyond immediate gains and invest in the long-term health of our communities and planet. Yet, the rewards are manifold—enhanced brand loyalty, differentiation in the market, and the satisfaction of contributing to the greater good.

As I reflect on this journey, I want to inspire others to view their businesses not just as commercial entities but as platforms for positive change. Patagonia and TOMS's examples, alongside our own initiatives, offer a blueprint for achieving this. They demonstrate that with creativity, commitment, and courage, businesses can thrive by doing good.

In conclusion, my journey through business and corporate generosity has reinforced my belief in the transformative power of ethical practices. It has shown me that the accurate measure of a brand's success lies in its financial achievements and its impact on the world. By championing ethical practices, businesses can enhance their brand image and contribute to a more just, sustainable, and compassionate world. This is the legacy I aspire to leave—a legacy defined not by what we acquire but by what we give back.

# 6

# Collaborating for Success: The Role of Reciprocity in Partnerships

I N THE TAPESTRY OF my professional journey, the threads of partnership and collaboration have woven patterns of success and learning that have shaped the fabric of my career. Reflecting on the past year, a chapter emerges, marked by a venture into the unknown—a partnership that was as risky as it was promising. The story of this collaboration is not just a narrative of business strategy but a testament to the power of mutual respect and reciprocity.

The decision to partner with another consultant, someone whose reputation preceded them yet remained a stranger to me in many ways, was akin to setting sail in uncharted waters. Our first encounter was shrouded in skepticism and hope, a delicate dance of professional courtesies masked by the undercurrent of doubt. As Helen Keller profoundly stated, "Alone we can do so little; together we can do so much." This quote, though not known to me at the outset, encapsulates the essence of our partnership.

The initial days were fraught with the challenges of aligning our visions, understanding each other's strengths, and navigating the uncertainties of any new alliance. It was a period of adjustment, where each interaction served as a brushstroke on the canvas of our partnership, gradually painting a picture of mutual respect and understanding.

Our turning point came through a series of open conversations, during which we laid bare our apprehensions and aspirations. During these dialogues, the concept of reciprocity took root in our collaboration. We began to appreciate the unique value each brought to the table, recognizing that our combined efforts could address the specific needs of our clients in ways we had not initially imagined.

As our partnership evolved, so did our relationship. What started as a cautious alliance transformed into a dynamic synergy driven by a foundation of mutual respect and reciprocity. Challenges that once seemed insurmountable became opportunities for innovation as we learned to leverage our complementary skills. The results were nothing short of remarkable, with our collaborative projects meeting and exceeding our clients' expectations.

This partnership journey, though specific in its context, reflects a universal truth about the nature of collaboration. Like a flashback to the trials and triumphs of past ventures, it serves as a reminder that the success of any alliance hinges on the willingness to listen, understand, and reciprocate. It foreshadows a future where collaborations rooted in these principles can transcend the sum of their parts, creating outcomes as impactful as they are enduring.

The backdrop of this narrative is set against the increasing importance of corporate partnerships in driving innovation and sustainability. In a world where challenges are complex and interconnected, the ability to forge effective alliances has become a cornerstone of business strategy. A study by Harvard Business Review underscores this reality, revealing that 80% of executives believe partnerships and alliances are essential to their growth strategy. This statistic validates the significance of collaboration and highlights the shifting paradigms of business success in the modern era.

As I reflect on the transformative power of this partnership, I am reminded of the imagery of a bridge—connecting two distinct shores, enabling passage where once there was an impasse. This bridge, built on the pillars of mutual respect and reciprocity, stands as a testament to the notion that true collaboration is about more than just shared goals; it's about shared values and the recognition that together, we can achieve so much more than we can alone.

In the following chapters, we will delve deeper into the value of reciprocal partnerships, exploring the strategies for building and maintaining successful collaborations, navigating the challenges that arise, and celebrating the achievements of working together. Through this exploration, we aim to uncover the essence of cooperation and its role in shaping successful, sustainable, and fulfilling business ventures.

## The Value of Reciprocal Partnerships - Why they matter in today's business world.

In the labyrinth of today's business world, where paths often diverge towards solitary pursuits of success, the value of reciprocal partnerships emerges like a beacon, guiding toward a realm where collaboration reigns supreme. My journey into the heart of such a partnership has illuminated the profound truth that, in unity, there is strength—a strength capable of fostering growth, innovation, and synergy that transcends the capabilities of the solitary traveler.

The inception of my partnership, cloaked in uncertainty, gradually unfurled to reveal the manifold benefits that reciprocal relationships harbor. It became evident that by merging our distinct strengths, resources, and visions, we could carve out new avenues of opportunity, access untapped markets, and cater to a broader spectrum of client needs. This collaboration, rooted in the shared ethos of mutual benefit, allowed us to leverage each other's expertise in a dance of complementary skills that propelled us towards common goals.

As the narrative of our partnership unfolded, it dawned upon me that the essence of these alliances lay not just in the pooling of resources but in the sharing of knowledge. Each discussion and shared challenge became a conduit for learning, a chance to view problems through a different lens and discover innovative solutions that neither of us could have conceived alone. This exchange, akin to the cross-pollination of ideas, nurtured a fertile ground for creativity and innovation, driving us to explore new horizons and push the boundaries of what we deemed possible.

Moreover, the efficiency gleaned from this partnership was palpable. By dividing responsibilities based on strengths, we optimized our workflow, reducing redundancies and streamlining processes. This led to cost savings and allowed us to expedite our deliverables, enhancing our responsiveness to client needs and elevating our competitive edge in the bustling marketplace.

Yet, perhaps the most profound realization was the sense of camaraderie and shared purpose that this partnership fostered. In a world often marked by competition and isolation, finding a like-minded ally to share the journey was refreshing and empowering. This alliance reminded me that, at its core, business is about human connections—about finding common ground and working together towards a vision that extends beyond individual success to encompass a collective triumph.

Reflecting on the tapestry of today's business environment, it's clear that the terrain is rapidly evolving, with innovation and sustainability at the forefront of global discourse. The increasing importance of corporate partnerships in addressing these complex challenges underscores the necessity of collaboration. As businesses strive to navigate the intricacies of technological advancements, environmental stewardship, and societal expectations, the ability to form and nurture reciprocal partnerships becomes indispensable.

A study by Harvard Business Review resonates deeply with this perspective, stating that 80% of executives believe partnerships and alliances are crucial to their growth strategy. This statistic not only validates the strategic importance of collaboration but also highlights a shifting paradigm—one that recognizes the power of unity in achieving not just business growth but also in contributing to a more sustainable and innovative future.

In this light, my partnership, once a venture into the unknown, now stands as a microcosm of the broader potential that reciprocal alliances hold. It serves as a testament to the idea that we can do so much more than we can alone. This chapter of my journey, enriched by the experiences and lessons gleaned from this collaboration, has instilled a renewed appreciation for the value of partnership in today's business world.

As we forge ahead, the narrative of reciprocal partnerships offers a compelling blueprint for success. This success is not measured solely by financial gain but by the richness of collaboration, the innovation it spawns, and the shared journey toward achieving a greater good. It is a reminder that in the tapestry of business, the threads of partnership and reciprocity are among the most vibrant, weaving patterns of success that are as enduring as they are beautiful.

# Building and Maintaining Successful Partnerships - Key strategies for effective collaboration.

Embarking on creating successful partnerships, I've come to understand that it's akin to navigating a river whose waters are both nurturing and challenging. Though fraught with uncertainties at the outset, the journey with my fellow consultant became a masterclass in crafting collaborations that survive and thrive. The essence of building and maintaining these partnerships lies in a symphony of strategies, each note playing a crucial role in the harmony of effective collaboration.

Clear communication emerged as the cornerstone of our alliance. Like a lighthouse guiding ships through the fog, open and honest dialogue ensured we navigated the initial uncertainties with a sense of direction. Through this transparency, we aligned our goals and expectations, setting a course for a partnership based on mutual understanding rather than assumptions. This dialogue was not a one-time concerto but an ongoing exchange, adapting and evolving as our collaboration grew.

Trust, the bedrock upon which our collaboration was built, was cultivated with patience and care. It blossomed from the seeds of reliability and mutual respect, watered by our consistent actions and commitment to our shared objectives. This trust was more than just a belief in each other's abilities; it was a deep-rooted confidence in our shared vision and the ethical compass that guided our decisions. In the garden of our partnership, trust was the soil that nourished every other aspect of our collaboration.

Flexibility became our compass, allowing us to navigate the inevitable challenges and changes accompanying our journey. Like a tree bending in the wind, we learned the importance of adapting to new circumstances without losing our core essence. This agility was crucial in overcoming obstacles, enabling us to pivot our strategies when needed and embrace new opportunities with an open mind.

The strategy of regular evaluation and feedback acted as our map and sextant, guiding us through the uncharted territories of our partnership. By setting aside time to reflect on our progress and address areas for improvement, we ensured that our collaboration continued to grow stronger and more effective. This process was not just about critiquing but about learning from each encounter and project and using those lessons to enhance our future endeavors.

Lastly, celebrating achievements together became the rhythm that drove our partnership forward. These moments of recognition and appreciation were not merely ceremonial but an acknowledgment of our joint efforts and successes. Whether it was a significant milestone or a small victory, taking the time to celebrate these achievements reinforced the bonds of our collaboration, infusing our partnership with a sense of unity and shared pride.

In the tapestry of my professional experiences, the partnership with my fellow consultant vividly illustrates the power of collaboration. It has shown me that the keys to building and maintaining successful partnerships are not grand gestures but everyday actions that demonstrate commitment, respect, and a shared desire to achieve greatness.

As I reflect on this chapter of my journey, I am reminded of Helen Keller's words: "Alone, we can do so little; together, we can do so much." This partnership, born out of a leap of faith, has become a living embodiment of that principle. It serves as a beacon for future collaborations, a reminder that when we join forces with others who share our vision and values, the potential for success is boundless.

In business, where the landscapes are ever-changing and the challenges often daunting, collaboration remains a constant source of strength and innovation. My journey with my fellow consultant has enriched my professional life and left an indelible mark on my understanding of what it truly means to collaborate for success. It is a testament to the fact that when we weave the threads of reciprocity, respect, and shared purpose into the fabric of our partnerships, the tapestry that emerges is one of enduring beauty and strength.

## Overcoming Challenges in Partnerships - Dealing with conflicts and misunderstandings.

Navigating through the complex web of partnership dynamics, I've learned that the journey is fraught with challenges that test the resilience and strength of the bond between collaborators. Like a vessel on turbulent seas, partnerships are vulnerable to conflicts and misunderstandings. Yet, it's in navigating these rough waters that the true depth of a partnership is revealed and fortified.

In my own voyage of collaboration, conflicts were not just bumps on the road but opportunities for growth and understanding. The first sign of discord felt like a gust of wind threatening to veer us off course. Doubts and misunderstandings, like shadows in the twilight, clouded our once-clear vision. It was a pivotal moment that demanded not just attention but action grounded in mutual respect and the foundation of reciprocity that underpinned our alliance.

The key to overcoming these challenges lies in open and honest communication. Initiating these conversations was akin to opening the windows during a storm, daunting yet necessary to clear the air. We approached these discussions not as adversaries but as allies with a shared purpose. By laying bare our concerns, expectations, and frustrations, we created a space where vulnerabilities were acknowledged, and solutions emerged from the synergy of our combined perspectives.

Active listening played a pivotal role in these dialogues. It required silencing my own preconceptions and truly hearing my partner's viewpoint. This act of empathy, of stepping into the other's shoes, was transformative. It shifted our discussions from a battleground of egos to a collaborative effort to find common ground. Through active listening, we unearthed the roots of our conflicts, often finding them misalignments in communication or differences in approach rather than insurmountable obstacles.

Collaboratively seeking solutions became our mantra. Compromise, though sometimes challenging, was necessary to align our diverse perspectives toward a unified solution. We learned to leverage our differences, turning them from sources of conflict into wellsprings of innovation. Finding common ground and blending our visions into a coherent strategy was challenging and rewarding. It was a dance of give and take, underpinned by the mutual respect that was the cornerstone of our partnership.

Preemptively, we established clear guidelines and protocols for conflict resolution, a lighthouse guiding us through the fog of future disagreements. These frameworks provided a structured approach to navigating conflicts, ensuring we had a map to find our way back to the collaborative ground even in the heat of disagreement.

Acknowledging mistakes and learning from them became a shared journey of growth. Each misstep and error was not a point of contention but a step towards a more profound understanding and strengthening of our partnership. This ethos of continual improvement, of recognizing that the path of collaboration is one of learning and adaptation, has been pivotal in navigating the challenges that arise.

As I reflect on this chapter of our partnership, I am struck by the paradox that the challenges we faced, the conflicts and misunderstandings, were not detriments but catalysts for strengthening our bond. They compelled us to engage more deeply, to understand more fully, and to commit more resolutely to our shared vision.

In navigating the complexities of collaboration, I've learned that overcoming partnership challenges is not just about resolving conflicts but transforming them into opportunities for growth, understanding, and deeper connection. This journey, marked by storms and calm seas alike, has taught me that the true strength of a partnership lies not in the absence of conflict but in the ability to overcome it together, emerging more vital, more aligned, and more committed to the shared path ahead.

In this narrative of overcoming challenges, I see not just the story of my partnership but a reflection of the broader truth underlying all successful collaborations. It's a testament to the power of mutual respect, open communication, and the unwavering belief that together, we can navigate any storm and reach the shores of success.

## Celebrating Success Together - How to jointly celebrate achievements and milestones.

In the collaboration journey, the moments of triumph and achievement hold a special place, akin to the golden hours at dawn after a long night's voyage. In my experience, celebrating success together is not merely a ceremonial act but a vital reinforcement of the bonds forged through shared endeavors and challenges. It's a practice that has imbued our partnership with camaraderie and mutual appreciation, turning milestones into shared treasures.

The act of jointly celebrating achievements has always been a pivotal chapter in the story of our collaboration. Each success, whether a project delivered beyond expectations or a hurdle overcome through joint effort, became a cause for celebration. These moments of recognition and appreciation were not just about acknowledging the outcome but honoring the journey—the perseverance, the innovation, and the shared vision that guided us to our goals.

Public recognition of individual contributions within the framework of our collective success became a tradition. It was a way to shine a light on the unique strengths each of us brought to the table, fostering a culture of appreciation and respect. This practice of acknowledgment went beyond the confines of our partnership, extending into the broader community of stakeholders, clients, and teams who supported our endeavors.

It was our way of saying, "Together, we achieve more," a mantra that resonated deeply within and beyond our immediate circle.

Celebratory events, from informal gatherings to more structured ceremonies, punctuated our journey. These events were imbued with a sense of unity and shared pride, whether held in the warmth of a shared meal or through the virtual connections that have become a staple of our times. They were occasions for reflection, laughter, and reaffirming our commitment to our shared path. In these gatherings, stories of challenges and triumphs were shared, weaving the individual threads of our experiences into a tapestry of collective achievement.

Sharing our success stories internally and through social media became a way to broadcast our journey to a broader audience. It served multiple purposes: inspiring our teams, engaging our clients, and attracting like-minded partners and collaborators. These narratives of success, framed through the lens of collaboration and mutual respect, served as beacons to others in the business community, illustrating the tangible benefits of partnership and reciprocal respect.

Moreover, setting aside time to reflect on the milestones reached and planning for the future became an integral part of our celebrations. These strategic sessions, often infused with the energy and optimism generated by our achievements, allowed us to dream bigger, set higher goals, and reinforce our commitment to our partnership. It was a process of looking back to appreciate how far we had come and looking forward to charting the course for our continued journey together.

By celebrating success together, we have strengthened the bonds of our partnership and cultivated a shared identity marked by resilience, innovation, and a commitment to excellence. This practice has reminded us that while the achievements are significant, the journey—the moments of doubt, the challenges overcome, and the lessons learned—truly defines our collaboration.

As I reflect on the impact of celebrating our successes together, I am reminded of the profound words of Helen Keller: "Alone we can do so little; together we can do so much." This principle, which has guided our partnership from its inception, finds its fullest expression in the moments we choose to celebrate our achievements. It underscores the truth that our successes are not merely the result of individual effort but the culmination of shared vision, mutual respect, and the unwavering belief in the power of collaboration.

In sharing this narrative, I hope to inspire others to recognize the value of celebrating achievements together, not as a formality but as a foundational element of successful partnerships. Through these celebrations, we not only honor our accomplishments but also reaffirm our commitment to the journey ahead, fortified by the bonds of collaboration and the shared joy of our achievements.

# Conclusion

As I stand at the crossroads of reflection and foresight, the journey of collaboration, with its myriad challenges and triumphs, unfolds like a well-thumbed map, each crease and fold a testament to the lessons learned and the distances traversed. The narrative of our partnership, marked by mutual respect, reciprocity, and shared celebrations, has illuminated the path to success and charted a course for future ventures. In this concluding section, I seek to distill the essence of our experiences into a compass for navigating the waters of collaborative endeavors, offering a reflection on our journey and actionable steps for those embarking on their own.

## The Symphony of Collaboration

Reflecting on the tapestry of our partnership, it becomes evident that the harmony achieved was not a product of chance but of intentional, concerted effort. The melody of our collaboration was composed of the notes of open communication, trust, flexibility, and mutual respect—each note essential, contributing to a symphony that resonated with the promise of shared success. The crescendos of our achievements and the diminuendos of our challenges were navigated with a conductor's precision, guided by the baton of our shared vision.

This journey has reaffirmed Helen Keller's timeless adage: "Alone we can do so little; together we can do so much."

The power of partnership, rooted in the fertile ground of reciprocity, can elevate individual aspirations into collective triumphs. It is a dance of give-and-take, where the steps are guided by the rhythms of mutual respect and the shared joy of achievement.

## Action Steps: Charting the Course Together

For those at the helm of their own collaborative vessels, seeking to navigate the seas of partnership, I offer these actionable steps gleaned from the depths of our experiences:

1. **Establish Open Channels of Communication:** From the outset, prioritize clear, honest communication. Let it be the compass that guides your partnership, ensuring that all parties are aligned in their objectives and expectations.

2. **Cultivate Trust Through Transparency:** Trust is the keel that keeps the partnership steady. Build it through actions that demonstrate reliability, transparency, and integrity. Let every interaction be a brick in the edifice of trust you seek to construct.

3. **Embrace Flexibility:** The waters of collaboration are ever-changing. Be prepared to adjust your sails to adapt your strategies and roles as the journey unfolds. Flexibility is the rudder that will steer you through unforeseen challenges.

4. **Engage in Regular Reflection and Feedback:** Set aside time for reflection, evaluation of the journey, acknowledgment of milestones reached, and charting the course forward. This practice is the sextant by which you can navigate the stars of your shared aspirations.

5. **Celebrate success Together:** Let the celebration of achievements be the wind in your sails, propelling you forward. Recognize and honor the contributions of each partner, for it is in the shared joy of success that the bonds of collaboration are strengthened.

6. **Commit to Continuous Learning and Growth:** View every challenge as an opportunity to learn, refine your approach, and deepen your partnership. The journey of collaboration is one of perpetual growth, where the lessons of the past illuminate the path to future success.

7. **Foster a Culture of Reciprocity:** Let the principle of give-and-take be the guiding star of your partnership. Approach each decision, each challenge, and each success with the mindset of mutual benefit, ensuring that the fruits of your collaboration are shared equitably.

In sharing these reflections and action steps, I hope to light a beacon for those embarking on their collaboration journeys.

The path is marked by challenges and triumphs, but it is worth treading, for the destinations reachable through the partnership are boundless.

As I gaze towards the horizon, the lessons of our collaboration serving as both anchor and compass, I am filled with anticipation for the adventures. For in the business world, as in life, it is through our connections with others that we find our greatest strength, most profound sources of inspiration, and most enduring successes.

Let us then step forward with confidence, guided by the principles of reciprocity and mutual respect, ready to embrace the infinite possibilities that collaboration unfolds. Together, we can chart a course to success for ourselves and the communities we serve, building a legacy of partnership that endures long after our individual journeys have merged into the collective voyage of progress.

# 7

# Turning Listening into a Competitive Advantage

DIVING INTO THE HEART of leadership and business innovation, I've realized that one of the most transformative powers at our disposal often goes unnoticed: the art of listening. It's a skill that, when mastered, can turn the tides of fortune in our favor, offering a competitive advantage that is both profound and sustainable. My journey into understanding this began not in the boardroom but rather in a place as ordinary as a dental office's front lobby. This experience illuminated for me the sheer impact that genuine listening can have on customer satisfaction and the very fabric of business success.

Reflecting on Dale Carnegie's timeless wisdom in "How to Win Friends and Influence People," I've seen firsthand how empathy and understanding—core tenets of effective listening—can forge deeper connections with those around us. Carnegie's insights were not just theoretical musings but practical strategies that have withstood the test of time, advocating for the profound impact of truly hearing and valuing others' perspectives.

This revelation hit me during a routine visit to one of my dental offices, intended for a simple customer service training session. However, I observed a stark reminder of how easy it is to miss the mark on genuine connection. Witnessing a dental assistant's automated response to a patient's heartfelt sharing about his dog's passing was a jarring wake-up call. It was a clear missed opportunity for genuine human connection, spotlighting the routine automation that often plagues our interactions. This instance was not isolated but indicative of a widespread issue where the essence of listening is overshadowed by the rush of procedural tasks.

The realization led me to innovate within the dental office, breaking away from the industry's standardized flow of patient interaction. Introducing a model where dentists engaged with patients right from the lobby, dedicating moments to non-dental conversation, opened new avenues for connection and understanding. This disruption enhanced patient relations and resulted in a staggering 79% increase in same-day dentistry starts—a testament to the power of listening and engaging on a more personal level.

The importance of this approach was further underscored by the rise of social listening in marketing strategies, highlighting a global recognition of listening as a crucial component of customer engagement and satisfaction. Statistics from Salesforce indicate that 89% of business customers expect companies to understand their needs and expectations, and the call for businesses to elevate their listening game has never been louder.

Our strategy focused on open-ended, "double-clicking" questions beyond surface-level inquiries, encouraging patients to share what mattered to them. This approach deepened our understanding of our patients' needs and mirrored the broader principle of reciprocity that I advocate for in "Profit with Purpose." We received loyalty, trust, and a strengthened business in return for giving our attention and understanding.

As we delve deeper into the subsequent sections, we will explore the art of listening in business, effective techniques for enhancing listening skills, how listening can drive innovation, and case studies of businesses that have thrived by prioritizing this skill. Each aspect will build on the foundation laid by this personal anecdote, demonstrating the universal value of listening across various facets of business and leadership.

This journey is not just about transforming our business practices but revolutionizing how we connect with those we serve and work alongside. By turning listening into a competitive advantage, we open ourselves to opportunities, insights, and innovations that can propel our businesses to new heights. Let's embark on this path together, redefining success through the power of genuine, reciprocal engagement.

# The Art of Listening in Business - Understanding its impact and value.

The art of listening in business transcends mere silence during another's speech; it is the foundation of genuine understanding and engagement and, ultimately, the cornerstone of profound leadership and innovation. Reflecting on my journey and the lessons from many experiences, I appreciate the multifaceted impact that listening can wield within business and beyond.

At its core, listening serves as a bridge between thought and action, where the silent pauses between words become the canvas for empathy, innovation, and connection. In these moments of attentiveness, the true needs, desires, and aspirations of employees, clients, and stakeholders emerge, offering insights that, when acted upon, can transform mere transactions into lasting relationships.

I've observed, both within my own businesses and through the experiences shared by others, how a culture steeped in the principles of active listening fosters an environment where trust flourishes and creativity thrives. It's a realm where every voice feels valued, where the hierarchy flattens into a landscape of mutual respect and collaborative pursuit. The benefits of cultivating such a culture are manifold, echoing through the corridors of productivity, engagement, and, ultimately, the bottom line.

But listening, especially in the bustling business world, requires more than passive presence; it demands intentionality and skill. It begins with the conscious decision to be fully present, casting aside the distractions that vie for our attention and truly immersing ourselves in the speaker's perspective. This level of engagement is not just about hearing words but about understanding the emotions, motivations, and unspoken messages that those words convey.

The practice of active listening, complemented by reflective listening and empathetic engagement techniques, becomes a powerful tool in our arsenal. By echoing what we've heard and asking questions that delve deeper, we signal our genuine interest and commitment to understanding. This enriches our insights and empowers those we engage with, validating their thoughts and feelings in a world that often seems too busy to care.

In my journey, from the dental office lobby to the boardrooms of businesses striving for growth, the implementation of listening strategies has been transformative. It's led to unveiling unmet needs, the birth of innovative solutions, and the strengthening of bonds that transcend the transactional nature of business. Through listening, we've uncovered opportunities for growth and pathways to solutions previously obscured by the noise of routine operations.

As leaders, our mission extends beyond implementing strategies; it's about embodying the essence of listening in every interaction, every decision, and every moment of connection. By doing so, we not only enhance the operational efficiency of our businesses but also sow the seeds for a legacy of impactful leadership, one that is remembered not for the noise it made but for the silence it honored and the understanding it fostered.

In the following sections, we will delve into specific techniques for enhancing listening skills, explore how listening can drive innovation, and examine case studies of businesses that have thrived by prioritizing listening. Each of these facets will build upon the foundational understanding that listening is not merely a skill to be acquired but a principle to be lived.

As we continue on this journey together, I invite you to reflect on the role that listening plays in your own life and leadership. By embracing the art of listening, we unlock the potential to transform our businesses and the lives of those we serve and lead. Let us step forward with the resolve to listen deeply, understand fully, and act wisely, charting a course toward a future marked by empathy, innovation, and lasting impact.

## Techniques for Effective Listening - Practical methods to enhance listening skills.

Embarking on the next phase of our journey, we delve into the techniques that amplify our listening capacity—a skill pivotal for fostering meaningful connections and driving business growth. Through my narrative, I aim to unravel the essence of effective listening, drawing upon personal insights and recognized strategies that underscore its significance in leadership and innovation.

Active listening is at the forefront of these techniques. It's a practice where one's focus is on the speaker, absorbing every word, tone, and unspoken emotion conveyed. This isn't passive hearing but an engaged and conscious effort to understand the message fully. Reflecting back, asking probing questions, and acknowledging the speaker's points without immediate judgment or response are hallmarks of this approach. It transforms conversations, making them richer and more insightful.

Another invaluable technique is reflective listening, which goes hand in hand with active listening. It involves paraphrasing or summarizing what the speaker has said to demonstrate understanding and clarify and delve deeper into the subject matter. This method fosters a profound level of engagement, ensuring that both parties are on the same page and that the listener has genuinely grasped the nuances of the speaker's message.

Empathy is another cornerstone of effective listening. It requires putting ourselves in the speaker's shoes and attempting to understand their perspective, emotions, and motivations without bias or preconception. This empathetic stance enhances the quality of our interactions and builds trust and rapport, creating a foundation for stronger, more resilient relationships.

In my quest to enhance the listening culture within my business ventures, I've emphasized minimizing distractions—a simple yet often overlooked aspect. In today's digital age, the constant pings of notifications can fracture attention and detract from the quality of interactions. Encouraging a policy of undivided attention during conversations, whether in person or virtually, has significantly improved the depth and productivity of our communications.

Asking open-ended questions that encourage detailed responses rather than yes/no answers has also been a game-changer. This technique invites elaboration, offering insights into thoughts, feelings, and ideas that might not emerge through more direct inquiries. It's a way to explore the breadth of a topic, uncovering layers that may not be immediately apparent.

Reflecting on these strategies, it becomes evident that listening is a skill to be cultivated and a gift to be shared. It's about more than just business outcomes; it's about human connection. Investing in our listening abilities opens doors to understanding, innovation, and mutual respect—qualities that underpin successful leadership and sustainable business growth.

As we progress, let us carry forward the lessons of active and reflective listening, empathy, and mindfulness amidst distractions. These are not merely techniques but principles to live by, guiding us toward becoming better leaders, innovators, and, most importantly, better humans.

## Listening and Innovation - How listening leads to innovative solutions and services.

In business and leadership, listening is not merely a passive act but a dynamic force that catalyzes innovation and creativity. My understanding of this transformative power deepened through experiences where listening acted as the key to unlocking novel solutions and services, reshaping how I approached challenges and opportunities.

Listening with intent and openness has allowed me to capture customers' and team members' unvoiced needs and desires, turning these insights into the bedrock of innovation within my ventures. This process, akin to social listening strategies in marketing, involves not just the collection of feedback but the active interpretation and application of this information to drive change and development.

One of the most enlightening moments in my career came when I realized that listening could lead to innovation by identifying gaps in the market. By attentively understanding customer complaints and suggestions, I was able to pinpoint areas where our services could evolve or where entirely new offerings could be introduced, significantly enhancing our competitive edge. This approach fostered a continuous improvement and adaptation culture, where every team member felt empowered to contribute ideas and feedback, knowing it would be heard and valued.

Moreover, embracing diversity in thought and experience within the team has nurtured a fertile ground for innovation. Actively listening to a wide range of perspectives has often led to the breakthrough of traditional boundaries, uncovering unique approaches to problem-solving and creativity. This diversity of input, catalyzed by a genuine commitment to understanding and valuing each voice, has propelled our ventures into uncharted territories of growth and success.

Incorporating feedback loops into the fabric of our operations has also been a crucial element in leveraging listening for innovation. These loops provide continuous streams of actionable insights and reinforce the value we place on the voices of those we serve and collaborate with. It's a testament to our commitment to not just hear but to listen and act, fostering a deep sense of trust and loyalty among customers and team members alike.

Reflecting on the journey thus far, it's clear that listening transcends the conventional boundaries of communication when done with intention, empathy, and openness. It becomes a powerful catalyst for innovation, driving businesses forward in their quest for excellence and impact. As we look ahead, the lessons gleaned from listening promise to lead us toward more meaningful, innovative, and sustainable pathways of growth and success.

The narrative of innovation through listening resonates across industries and sectors, urging leaders and entrepreneurs to embrace the silent strength of attentiveness. It challenges us to listen not just to respond but to understand and innovate, paving the way for a future where businesses thrive not just on the brilliance of their ideas but on the depth of their understanding.

## Case Studies - Businesses that have thrived by prioritizing listening.

As we delve into real-world applications of the principles we've discussed, I'm reminded of the transformative power of listening in business. Through my journey and observations, I've witnessed firsthand how businesses that prioritize listening have thrived and set new benchmarks for success and innovation. The stories of Zappos and Airbnb stand out as beacons of what can be achieved when listening is placed at the heart of business strategy.

Zappos, renowned for its unparalleled customer service, has always understood the value of listening to its customers. By actively seeking feedback and genuinely engaging with customer needs and experiences, Zappos has crafted a brand synonymous with service excellence. This commitment to listening has fostered deep loyalty among its customers and propelled the company to the forefront of the e-commerce space. It's a clear testament to how a culture of listening can translate into tangible business success.

Similarly, Airbnb's ascension in the hospitality industry is a narrative of innovation fueled by attentive listening. By creating a platform that encourages open dialogue between hosts and guests, Airbnb has tapped into its community's real needs and preferences. This approach has enabled the company to continuously refine and expand its offerings, ensuring they remain relevant and highly valued by users worldwide. Airbnb's story highlights the potential of listening to drive growth, transform industries, and redefine the parameters of customer satisfaction.

These case studies underscore a fundamental truth: businesses that listen—to their customers, employees, and the market at large—are businesses that lead. They exemplify how the art of listening can be harnessed to foster innovation, cultivate loyalty, and achieve unprecedented success. As leaders and entrepreneurs, these examples offer invaluable insights into the potential of embracing the power of listening as a strategic cornerstone.

As we conclude this exploration of listening as a competitive advantage, let us carry forward the lessons learned from these pioneering companies. The ongoing listening journey offers endless opportunities for growth, connection, and transformation. Let us commit to being listeners at every level of our organizations and, in doing so, unlock the boundless potential that lies in understanding and responding to the voices that matter most.

## Conclusion and Action Steps

Reflecting on our journey through the transformative power of listening, we've uncovered its pivotal role in driving business innovation, fostering strong relationships, and leading to unprecedented success. From the personal anecdotes shared to the illustrative examples of Zappos and Airbnb, the message is clear: listening is not merely a passive activity but a strategic tool that can set businesses apart in a competitive landscape.

As we conclude this exploration, I am compelled to leave you with actionable steps that encapsulate the essence of our discussion. These steps are designed to encourage reflection and prompt tangible change within your leadership approach and organizational culture.

1. **Institute Regular Feedback Loops:** Implement mechanisms for receiving and acting on feedback from customers and employees. This could involve surveys, suggestion boxes, or regular open forums.

2. **Practice Active and Reflective Listening:** Engage fully in conversations, reflecting on what you've heard to ensure understanding and deepen the connection with the speaker.

3. **Cultivate a Culture of Empathy:** Encourage your team to put themselves in others' shoes, understanding

their perspectives and needs deeply, to foster a more inclusive and supportive environment.

4. **Minimize Distractions in Communication:** Create spaces and norms prioritizing attentive listening, such as device-free meetings or designated 'listening sessions' with stakeholders.

5. **Train and Develop Listening Skills:** Offer workshops or training sessions to enhance your team's listening abilities, emphasizing the importance of this skill in building relationships and driving innovation.

As we part ways from this chapter, I invite you to embrace these steps as a pathway to better business outcomes and a more profound, empathetic, and effective leadership style. Let the power of listening be your guide to unlocking the potential within your team, your customers, and, ultimately, your business.

With this knowledge and these actionable steps, you can turn listening into a formidable competitive advantage, propelling your business toward new horizons of success and fulfillment.

# 8

# The Power of Saying 'Yes' to Community Involvement

As a business leader, my journey has been filled with countless lessons, strategies, and milestones. But among these myriad experiences, one philosophy has stood out as a beacon of transformative power: the spirit of giving back. It's a principle deeply rooted in the belief, as eloquently expressed by Mahatma Gandhi, that "The best way to find yourself is to lose yourself in the service of others." While timeless, this notion is especially poignant in today's business landscape, where the essence of reciprocity can unlock doors to growth and meaningful, sustainable success.

I recall watching "Pay It Forward" for the first time—a movie that encapsulates the profound impact of altruism through a simple yet powerful idea. The film's premise is not merely cinematic fiction but a tangible strategy that can foster an unparalleled depth of community connection and customer loyalty when applied to the business world. This realization dawned on me not through the pages of a business textbook but through a personal journey that underscored the value of community engagement.

Several years ago, I initiated a modest community project aiming to contribute to our local food bank. Though small in scale, this endeavor was a gesture of gratitude towards the community that had cradled my business since its inception. The outcome was unexpectedly profound. This simple act of giving opened new avenues for partnerships and growth and cemented my company's reputation as a bastion of community support. It taught me that people gravitate towards businesses that offer value and embody compassion and social responsibility.

But why, you might wonder, does community involvement hold such significance for businesses today? The answer lies in the fabric of modern society, where businesses are often perceived as impersonal entities focused solely on profit. By weaving community engagement into the core of your business strategy, you humanize your brand and build enduring relationships based on trust and mutual respect. This shift from transactional interactions to meaningful connections can transform customers into advocates and businesses into cornerstones of their communities.

In the forthcoming sections, we'll delve into the critical importance of community for businesses, unveiling how active engagement can bolster your brand and foster an environment of loyalty and support. We'll explore actionable strategies for embedding community participation into your business model, dissect the tangible and intangible rewards accompanying such involvement, and share inspirational success stories of businesses that have thrived by prioritizing community engagement.

Integrating the principle of reciprocity into your business ethos isn't merely about philanthropy; it's a strategic imperative that enhances your brand's value proposition. When your business practices reflect a genuine commitment to the community's well-being, you're not just selling a product or service but nurturing a legacy. This legacy transcends the conventional success metrics, embodying a profound commitment to societal growth and collective prosperity.

Through my own experiences, I've witnessed firsthand how a focus on community and reciprocity can elevate a business from a mere participant in the market to a leader, revered not just for its products or services but for its contribution to the greater good. Embedding these values into your business may challenge conventional norms and require a reevaluation of your strategies. Still, the rewards for your company and the community are immeasurable.

As we embark on this exploration, remember that the path to becoming a market leader is paved not just with profit but with purpose. It's a journey that demands more than strategic acumen; it calls for a heart willing to give, support, and transform. In the spirit of Gandhi's wisdom, let us lose ourselves in the service of others, for it is in giving that we truly find the path to unparalleled business success.

## The Heartbeat of Success: Why Community Matters

In my years at the helm of a thriving business, I've come to understand that the essence of true success lies not within the walls of corporate offices or the figures on balance sheets but in the heart of the community we serve. This realization was not instantaneous; it evolved through experiences, observations, and a deep-seated belief in the power of giving back. Business leaders often find ourselves engrossed in pursuing growth, scalability, and innovation. Yet, it is crucial to remember that our businesses do not exist in isolation. They are part of a larger ecosystem—a community that sustains and nurtures them.

The significance of community involvement for businesses is manifold and profound. It serves as the bridge that connects our corporate aspirations with the grassroots realities of the people we aim to serve. By engaging with the community, we do more than just build a brand; we foster a legacy of trust, loyalty, and mutual support. This reciprocal relationship between businesses and their communities is the cornerstone of sustainable growth and genuine leadership.

My journey toward embracing community involvement was sparked by a simple yet transformative project—a local initiative to support underprivileged families in our area. This endeavor, though modest in scope, opened my eyes to the impactful role businesses can play in addressing societal needs. The profound gratitude, goodwill, and sense of unity emanated from this project. It taught me that when businesses extend their reach beyond commerce and genuinely invest in community welfare, they unlock a reservoir of goodwill and respect that no marketing campaign could achieve.

Community involvement extends beyond social responsibility; it is a strategic imperative that can significantly enhance a business's competitive edge. Consumers are increasingly drawn to brands that commit to societal well-being in today's hyper-connected world. By actively participating in community initiatives, businesses contribute to the betterment of society and cultivate a positive brand image that resonates with customers on a deeper, more emotional level.

Moreover, community engagement fosters a sense of belonging and loyalty among employees. It allows them to contribute to meaningful causes, enhancing their job satisfaction and sense of purpose. This, in turn, boosts morale, productivity, and, ultimately, the business's overall performance. Furthermore, a strong community presence can attract top talent eager to work for companies that align with their values and aspirations.

However, meaningful community involvement requires more than just financial contributions. It demands a genuine understanding of the community's needs, aspirations, and challenges. Active listening, empathy, and open dialogue can only achieve this understanding. By engaging in conversations with community members, businesses can gain valuable insights into how best to serve and support their local ecosystems.

This section will explore various strategies for effective community engagement, emphasizing the importance of authenticity, collaboration, and long-term commitment. From supporting local charities and sponsoring community events to launching initiatives that address specific societal issues, the avenues for making a meaningful impact are vast and varied. No matter how small, each gesture of goodwill contributes to building a stronger, more resilient community.

As we delve deeper into the why and how of community involvement, remember that at the heart of every successful business lies a commitment to serve—not just the interests of shareholders but the well-being of the entire community. This holistic approach to business is not just the right thing to do but the smart thing. It is the foundation upon which lasting success is built, where every act of giving back is a step toward a more prosperous, equitable, and sustainable future for all.

By embracing the spirit of community, we elevate our businesses and enrich our lives and those around us. Let this section serve as a guide and an inspiration for integrating community involvement into your business ethos. Together, we can transform our businesses into powerful forces for good, creating ripples of positive change that extend far beyond our immediate surroundings.

# Crafting Bridges: Strategies for Effective Community Engagement

Navigating the path to effective community engagement has been both a challenge and a revelation in my journey as a business leader. I've learned that true engagement goes beyond mere participation; it's about crafting bridges that connect your business's heart with the community's soul. This realization didn't come overnight. It resulted from trial and error and the relentless pursuit of meaningful impact. Through this journey, I've discovered strategies that foster genuine connections and enhance our business's relevance and resonance within the community.

## 1. Listening with Intent

The first step toward impactful community engagement is listening—truly listening—to the voices within the community. It's easy to assume we understand their needs and aspirations, but the assumption is the mother of all missteps. I recall organizing our first community forum, a platform to facilitate open dialogue between our business and the local residents. The insights from this forum were eye-opening, revealing nuances of the community's needs we had previously overlooked. This experience underscored the importance of active listening and reinforced my belief that effective solutions are co-created, not imposed.

## 2. Partnering with Purpose

No business is an island, and this holds especially true regarding community engagement. Early on, I recognized the power of partnerships in amplifying our impact. By collaborating with local nonprofits, schools, and other businesses, we were able to pool resources, share expertise, and collectively address community challenges. These partnerships were not mere alliances but bonds forged on the shared commitment to making a tangible difference. One particularly successful initiative was a joint literacy program with a local library to improve access to education for underprivileged children. The success of this program highlighted the synergistic potential of purpose-driven partnerships.

## 3. Transparency and Trust

Building trust within the community is paramount, and transparency is its foundation. We committed to being open about our intentions, processes, and outcomes in every project we undertook. This approach fostered a culture of trust and encouraged community members to actively participate and take ownership of the initiatives. Trust, I learned, is not granted; it's earned through consistent, honest engagement and unwavering respect for the community's voice.

## 4. Sustainable Commitment

Effective community engagement is not a one-off campaign

or a seasonal project; it's a long-term commitment. It requires a sustainable approach that considers the community's future well-being. Our business adopted a philosophy of "engagement for growth," where every initiative is designed to foster community development and business growth. This sustainable approach ensures that our engagement efforts contribute to lasting positive change, creating a legacy of impact that transcends business cycles.

## 5. Celebrating Successes and Learning from Failures

Every community engagement journey is a mix of successes and setbacks. Celebrating the successes is crucial, not just for morale but also for demonstrating the tangible benefits of collaboration. Equally important is the willingness to learn from failures, to adapt and refine our strategies based on what doesn't work. I've found that sharing these learnings with the community enhances our strategies and strengthens our bond with the community, as they see us as a partner committed to continuous improvement.

As we delve into these strategies, remember that effective community engagement is a journey of discovery, learning, and growth. It's about creating value that transcends the confines of business and touches the lives of those in our community. By listening with intent, partnering with purpose, embracing transparency, committing to sustainability, and learning from every experience, we can forge meaningful connections that benefit our businesses and communities.

The next section will explore the tangible and intangible benefits of such deep-rooted community involvement. These benefits underscore the importance of engagement and highlight its role in shaping the future of our businesses and communities.

# The Ripple Effect: Benefits of Deep Community Involvement

Embarking on a journey of genuine community engagement has been one of the most rewarding endeavors in my career as a business leader. This path has enriched the communities we've partnered with and given my business many tangible and intangible benefits. Reflecting on this journey, it's clear that the impact of our community involvement extends far beyond philanthropy; it's a strategic investment that yields profound returns for our business and the community.

## Tangible Benefits: A Strengthened Business Foundation

The tangible benefits of deep community involvement are both immediate and measurable. Increased brand visibility is one such benefit that we've experienced firsthand. Our business name became synonymous with positive change by actively participating in community projects, leading to heightened brand awareness and recognition. This visibility, in turn, has translated into increased customer loyalty. Customers are more inclined to support businesses they perceive as contributors to their community's well-being, resulting in a loyal customer base that values our commitment to social responsibility.

Furthermore, our community engagement efforts have facilitated new business opportunities. We've expanded our network through partnerships and collaborations, opening doors to ventures and alliances previously beyond our reach. These opportunities have contributed to our bottom line and diversified our business portfolio, enhancing our resilience in a competitive market.

## Intangible Benefits: Cultivating a Legacy of Impact

While the tangible benefits are significant, the intangible benefits of community involvement have been transformative. The most profound of these is the enhancement of our business reputation. In today's digital age, a company's reputation is its most valuable asset. Our deep-rooted community involvement has established our business as a leader in social responsibility, setting us apart from competitors and elevating our standing in the business community.

Employee morale and engagement have also seen a remarkable uplift. When team members witness their efforts contributing to meaningful change, they feel a sense of pride and fulfillment that transcends the confines of the workplace. This enhanced morale has led to increased productivity and a vibrant, positive workplace culture, attracting top talent eager to be part of a purpose-driven organization.

However, the most significant intangible benefit is the profound sense of purpose and fulfillment we've gleaned from our community engagement. Knowing that our business practices make a real difference in people's lives provides satisfaction that surpasses any financial reward. This fulfillment has become a driving force for innovation and excellence, inspiring us to continue pushing the boundaries of what's possible in business and community partnerships.

## A Catalyst for Sustainable Growth

As we've navigated the complexities of community engagement, it's become evident that these endeavors are not just beneficial but essential for sustainable business growth. The synergy between our business and the community has created a virtuous cycle where each success fuels further innovation, collaboration, and impact. This dynamic relationship has propelled our business to new heights and contributed to the resilience and prosperity of the communities we serve.

In retrospect, the decision to deeply engage with our community has catalyzed transformation within our business and beyond. It has taught us that the potential for positive change is boundless when businesses and communities unite in the spirit of reciprocity and mutual growth. As we continue on this journey, we do so with the conviction that our community involvement is not just a part of our business strategy—it is the heartbeat of our success.

## Illuminating the Path: Success Stories of Community Engagement

As we've navigated the intricacies of community involvement, we've underscored its importance and outlined strategies to maximize its impact. Yet, the true essence of its value shines brightest through the stories of businesses that have embarked on this journey and reaped its rewards. These narratives serve as a testament to the power of community engagement and as beacons guiding us toward realizing its full potential within our own ventures.

## Patagonia: A Vanguard of Environmental Stewardship

Patagonia's commitment to the environment and community welfare shows how deeply ingrained values can shape a company's destiny. This outdoor apparel giant has woven environmental stewardship into every thread of its operations, most notably through its "1% for the Planet" pledge, donating 1% of its sales to environmental causes. But Patagonia's engagement doesn't stop at financial contributions; it actively participates in environmental advocacy and sustainability initiatives, rallying its community of customers and employees around a shared mission to protect our planet. The result? A brand that's not just admired for its products but revered for its ethos, fostering unparalleled brand loyalty and setting a benchmark for corporate responsibility.

## Starbucks: Brewing a Stronger Community

Starbucks' journey of community engagement offers a masterclass in leveraging corporate scale for positive impact. Beyond its global coffee empire lies a deep commitment to community service, as exemplified by its Community Store Program. This initiative transforms select Starbucks locations into hubs for community programs, job training, and social impact activities tailored to the local community's needs. Moreover, Starbucks' pledge to hire refugees and veterans underscores its dedication to inclusivity and social justice. Through these efforts, Starbucks has cultivated a brand identity that transcends the realm of retail, embedding itself into the social fabric of communities worldwide, enhancing its reputation, and forging deep connections with customers and employees alike.

## The Small Business Advantage: Local Impact, Global Inspiration

While global corporations like Patagonia and Starbucks showcase the scale of impact possible through community engagement, it's crucial to recognize small businesses' unique advantage in this arena. My own journey echoes this sentiment. As a leader of a smaller enterprise, our ability to pivot, personalize our efforts, and deeply integrate into the local community has allowed us to create significant, meaningful change. We've built a strong, loyal community base by focusing on initiatives that directly address local needs—sponsoring youth sports teams, participating in community clean-ups, or supporting local arts and education. This engagement has not only elevated our business profile. Still, it has also fostered a sense of belonging and purpose among our team, propelling us forward with a shared vision of success and community well-being.

## Emulating Success Through Authentic Engagement

The stories of Patagonia, Starbucks, and countless small businesses, including mine, underscore a universal truth: genuine, thoughtful community engagement is a powerful catalyst for business success. These narratives inspire us to look beyond the conventional confines of business operations and explore how we can contribute to the communities that sustain us. Whether you lead a global corporation or a local boutique, the principles of community involvement remain the same—listen, engage, partner, and commit to making a difference.

As we reflect on these success stories, let us draw inspiration from their achievements and challenges. The path to meaningful community engagement is paved with persistence, creativity, and a genuine desire to contribute to the greater good. By adopting a strategic approach to community involvement grounded in authenticity and mutual respect, we can amplify our business's impact and leave a lasting legacy of positive change.

## Charting the Course Forward: Conclusion and Action Steps

As we draw this chapter close, reflecting on the community engagement journey reveals a landscape of opportunities, challenges, and profound rewards. From the foundational principle espoused by Mahatma Gandhi, urging us to lose ourselves in the service of others, to the inspirational tales of businesses, large and small, a common thread emerges: the transformative power of giving back. This journey, illuminated by personal experiences and the success stories of others, has not only reinforced my belief in the importance of community involvement but also crystallized its pivotal role in building a legacy of positive impact and sustainable success.

### The Essence of Our Journey

Embracing community engagement requires more than a strategic shift; it demands a cultural transformation within our businesses. It's about aligning our corporate goals with the greater good, weaving the fabric of social responsibility into the very DNA of our operations. This alignment enhances our business's value proposition and elevates our contribution to society. As leaders, our commitment to community engagement reflects our vision for a business model that prioritizes reciprocity, fosters genuine connections and cultivates a legacy of positive change.

## Action Steps: Moving from Insight to Impact

I propose the following action steps to translate the insights gleaned from this chapter into tangible outcomes. These are designed to guide you, regardless of your business's size or scope, toward initiating or enhancing your community engagement journey.

## 1. Conduct a Community Needs Assessment:

Begin by understanding the unique needs and challenges of your community. Engage in dialogues, conduct surveys, or host forums to gather insights directly from community members and stakeholders. This initial step ensures that your engagement efforts are both relevant and impactful.

## 2. Develop a Strategic Community Engagement Plan:

Based on the needs assessment, outline a plan that aligns with your business's core values and competencies. Identify potential partnerships, set clear objectives, and establish metrics for measuring success. Remember, authenticity and commitment are key to creating a meaningful plan.

### 3. Foster Partnerships for Amplified Impact:

Seek out collaborations with local organizations, nonprofits, and other businesses. These partnerships can amplify your impact, share resources, and create a united front for addressing community challenges. Ensure that these collaborations are based on shared values and mutual respect.

### 4. Implement, Evaluate, and Adapt:

Launch your community engagement initiatives with a focus on transparency and inclusivity. Regularly evaluate the impact of these efforts, soliciting feedback from community members and your team. Be prepared to adapt your strategies based on this feedback, embracing continuous improvement as a core principle.

### 5. Celebrate and Share Your Journey:

Acknowledge and celebrate the successes of your community engagement efforts, no matter how small. Share these stories through your marketing channels, highlighting the collective achievements and learning experiences. This will bolster your brand and inspire others to embark on their own journeys of community engagement.

## A Call to Action: Join the Movement

As we conclude this chapter, I invite you, fellow business leaders and entrepreneurs, to join me in this movement of transformative community engagement. Let us seize this opportunity to redefine the role of business in society, moving beyond profit to purpose, from transactions to transformative relationships. By doing so, we contribute to our communities' prosperity and lay the groundwork for a legacy of meaningful success.

Let this chapter be your catalyst, igniting a passion for positive change and guiding you toward a harmonious future where business and community thrive together. The journey ahead is both a challenge and a privilege, and it begins with a single step: your commitment to making a difference. Together, we can chart a course toward a brighter, more inclusive future.

# 9

# Nurturing Customer Relationships with Reciprocal Marketing

I MAGINE STEPPING INTO A world where the cornerstone of your business isn't just about transactions but about creating a tapestry of meaningful connections. As a leader in the bustling corridors of commerce, I found myself constantly searching for that elusive strategy that would elevate my business and embed it deeply within the heart of every customer.

In my journey, I discovered a compelling concept tucked within the pages of Robert B. Cialdini's "Influence: The Psychology of Persuasion." It spoke of reciprocity, a powerful yet often overlooked principle that could redefine how businesses interact with customers. It was an 'aha' moment, realizing this wasn't just about giving to get but fostering a culture of mutual respect and value.

This revelation was further solidified by a classic cinematic tale, "Miracle on 34th Street," where the generosity of a department store, Santa Claus, not only won the hearts of the city but also drove unprecedented growth for the store. This movie, though fictional, highlighted the profound impact of prioritizing customer needs and the unexpected boons of giving without immediately expecting in return.

Drawing from these influences, I embarked on a personal quest within my own business, initiating a marketing campaign that was less about selling and more about giving back. It was a risky move, diverging from the conventional paths trodden by many. Yet, what we experienced was nothing short of miraculous. Not only did we see our customer engagement soar, but we also witnessed a remarkable uptick in customer loyalty and referrals. It was as if we had unlocked a secret door to sustainable growth by simply shifting our focus from profit to purpose.

Now, I want to share what I've learned and how you, too, can integrate the power of reciprocity into your business practices. This chapter delves deep into the art of reciprocal marketing, a strategy that champions mutual benefit. It's about creating a symbiotic relationship with your customers, where both parties feel valued and appreciated.

We'll explore the concept of reciprocal marketing, breaking down its principles and how it can transform how you think about customer relationships. From the initial understanding of its foundations, we'll journey together through the practical steps of implementing these strategies in your day-to-day operations. Through real-world examples and personal insights, I'll guide you in measuring the impact of your efforts and continuously refining your approach for maximum effectiveness.

But this chapter isn't just about strategies and theories. It's a testament to the profound shifts that can occur when businesses operate from a place of generosity and genuine care. It's about embracing a new paradigm where success is measured not just by the bottom line but by our positive impact on the lives of those we serve.

So, as we step into this exploration together, remember that the journey of transforming your business with reciprocity is as much about the destination as it is about the journey itself. It's a path of discovery, learning, and, ultimately, fulfillment as you find new ways to enrich your customers' lives and, in turn, watch as your business thrives like never before.

Welcome to the chapter on nurturing customer relationships with reciprocal marketing. Here, we'll unlock the secrets to creating a business that grows and flourishes through the power of giving back. Let's embark on this journey together, reshaping the future of our businesses and setting a new standard for success.

## The Concept of Reciprocal Marketing - Defining and understanding its principles.

Diving into the heart of reciprocal marketing, I realized it was more than just a strategy; it was a mindset shift. At its core, reciprocal marketing is built on the principle that mutual benefit and cooperation between a business and its customers pave the way for true growth. It's about creating a give-and-take relationship that goes beyond the transactional and delves into the transformative.

I first encountered this concept when I sought to redefine our marketing approach. We wanted to move away from traditional strategies that felt more like shouting into a void and instead foster a genuine and impactful connection. Reciprocal marketing became our north star, guiding us toward a more collaborative and mutually beneficial way of engaging with our audience.

The principles of reciprocal marketing are simple yet profound. They start with the understanding that every interaction with a customer is an opportunity to create value, not just for us but for them as well. This value doesn't always have to be tangible; it can be the feeling of being heard, understood, and appreciated. From there, it's about building on this foundation with deliberate and authentic actions, whether through shared content, collaborative projects, or simply lending an ear to their needs and feedback.

Implementing this strategy wasn't without its challenges. Identifying the right partners, for instance, required a deep dive into who could offer us the best exposure or resources and who shared our values and vision for creating a better customer experience. It was about finding those who were just as committed to the journey of mutual growth as we were.

The next step was crafting a framework for our reciprocal efforts. This involved clear, open communication and setting shared goals aligned with our vision. It was crucial to establish transparency and trust from the outset, ensuring that all parties felt valued and invested in the success of our collaborations.

As we embarked on this journey, the impact was immediate and multifaceted. We saw a boost in customer engagement and loyalty and witnessed how these reciprocal relationships fostered a sense of community around our brand. Customers were not just passive recipients of our services; they became active participants, sharing their experiences, offering insights, and even advocating on our behalf.

However, perhaps the most significant takeaway from our foray into reciprocal marketing was the lesson in humility and the power of giving without the immediate expectation of return. This approach has enriched our customer relationships and instilled a sense of purpose and fulfillment in our team. We've learned that by focusing on what we can give rather than what we can get, we unlock a level of abundance that transcends the bottom line.

Reflecting on this journey, I'm reminded of the countless stories of businesses and leaders who have embraced reciprocal marketing and seen their worlds transform. These stories are a testament to the fact that when we dare to give freely and foster genuine connections, the rewards are far greater and more lasting than we could ever imagine.

As we move forward, the principles of reciprocal marketing will continue to guide our efforts. We walk this path with our customers, one built on trust, respect, and a shared commitment to growth and success. I invite you to join us as we explore the boundless possibilities of what we can achieve together through the power of reciprocity.

## Implementing Reciprocal Strategies - Practical steps for integrating reciprocity in marketing.

With the foundational principles of reciprocal marketing firmly in place, the next step on our journey was to weave these strategies into the fabric of our daily operations. This phase was about turning theory into practice, crafting a blueprint for action that would bring our vision of mutual growth and collaboration to life.

The transition began with identifying potential partners who shared our ethos and had complementary strengths. This wasn't just about finding businesses with similar customer bases but about aligning with those who understood the value of giving as much as receiving. It was essential to approach these partnerships openly, setting the stage for a relationship based on trust and mutual benefit.

Once we found our partners, we defined the contours of our collaborative efforts. Clear, candid conversations laid the groundwork for these partnerships as we outlined our shared goals and the mechanisms to achieve them. This step was critical; it was where expectations were set, roles were assigned, and the blueprint for our joint endeavors was drawn.

Implementing our reciprocal marketing strategies was both exhilarating and challenging. We launched co-branded initiatives, cross-promotions, and joint events, each designed to amplify our collective reach while providing tangible value to our customers. These initiatives were not just about broadening our exposure; they were opportunities to deepen our relationships with our audience by offering them something unique and beneficial.

Throughout this process, communication was our lifeline. Regular check-ins with our partners ensured that our projects aligned with our original vision and allowed us to adjust our strategies as needed. These interactions were not just logistical; they were opportunities to learn from each other and strengthen our partnership.

The impact of these efforts was profound. We witnessed a significant increase in customer engagement as our audience resonated with the authenticity and value of our collaborative projects. Our brand visibility grew, not just through increased exposure but through the endorsement of our partners and the quality of what we were offering together.

Yet, the journey of implementing reciprocal marketing strategies taught us more than just the mechanics of collaboration. It reinforced the importance of genuine commitment to our customers and partners. This wasn't a short-term tactic but a long-term investment in building relationships rooted in mutual respect and shared success.

Reflecting on this phase of our journey, I'm reminded of the countless interactions with customers who were excited to see businesses working together for their benefit. Their enthusiasm was a clear indicator that we were on the right path, leading to business growth and a stronger, more connected community.

Our commitment to reciprocal marketing remains unwavering as we look to the future. It's a commitment that goes beyond transactions, reaching into the heart of what it means to be a business in today's world. It's about creating a legacy of generosity, collaboration, and shared success that will endure for generations.

So, as we continue to navigate the evolving business landscape, let us do so, knowing that our greatest achievements lie in the value we create for others. This is the essence of reciprocal marketing and the guiding light that will lead us to new heights of success and fulfillment.

## Measuring the Impact - Tools and techniques to assess the effectiveness of reciprocal marketing.

After launching our reciprocal marketing campaigns, the next crucial step was to measure their impact. This phase was about reveling in our successes and understanding the nuances of our strategies and how they resonated with our audience. It was a journey into the analytical, yet it felt deeply personal, as every piece of data offered insights into the lives and preferences of the people we served.

To embark on this evaluative journey, we turned to various tools and techniques designed to peel back the layers of our marketing efforts. We started by setting clear metrics for success, including sales figures and customer acquisition costs, engagement rates, customer satisfaction scores, and the depth of interaction with our content. These metrics were our north star, guiding our analysis and helping us to understand where our efforts were most effective.

We employed a mix of qualitative and quantitative methods to gather data. Customer surveys became a regular part of our feedback loop, offering invaluable insights directly from the people we aimed to serve. These surveys were complemented by analytics tools that tracked website traffic, social media engagement, and conversion rates, painting a comprehensive picture of our campaigns' reach and impact.

Perhaps one of the most enlightening aspects of this process was A/B testing. We refined our approach by experimenting with different messages, offers, and collaboration formats, tailoring our efforts to what truly resonated with our audience. This iterative process was not just about optimization; it was a dialogue with our customers, a way of asking them, without words, what they valued most.

The insights gained from these evaluations were eye-opening. We learned not just about the effectiveness of our strategies but also about the changing dynamics of customer preferences and the growing importance of authenticity and value in marketing. This understanding allowed us to pivot and adapt, ensuring that our reciprocal marketing efforts remained relevant and impactful.

Reflecting on this phase of our journey, I am struck by the power of data to inform and transform. Measuring the impact of our reciprocal marketing campaigns provided us with a roadmap for future initiatives, illuminating the path toward even greater connection and collaboration with our audience.

Our commitment to reciprocal marketing is stronger than ever as we move forward, armed with the knowledge and insights gained from this evaluative process. It's a commitment to continuous learning, adaptation, and, above all, to serving our customers with integrity and purpose. This journey has taught us that the true measure of our success lies not in the numbers but in the lives we touch and the communities we build.

## Real-World Examples - Successful reciprocal marketing campaigns and their outcomes.

As we journey deeper into the heart of reciprocal marketing, it becomes clear that success stories are not just found within our own endeavors but echoed across the business landscape.

These narratives inspire and serve as beacons, guiding us toward innovative approaches to fostering relationships and building communities.

One such story that profoundly influenced our path was the partnership between GoPro and Red Bull. This collaboration was a masterclass in leveraging shared values and audiences to create a marketing symphony that resonated across the globe. Their joint ventures, especially the iconic "Stratos" event, were about showcasing products and creating experiences that embodied the spirit of adventure and innovation. This partnership taught us the power of aligning with brands with a similar ethos and the incredible impact such alliances can have on customer engagement and brand perception.

Equally compelling was the collaboration between Uber and Spotify. This initiative allowed users to personalize their rides by playing their own Spotify playlists, transforming a simple journey into a personalized experience. This partnership highlighted the importance of integrating services to add value to the customer's daily life, a principle we took to heart in our reciprocal marketing efforts.

These examples served as a testament to the transformative power of reciprocal marketing when executed with creativity, authenticity, and a deep understanding of customer desires. They reinforced our belief in the strategy's potential to drive business growth and forge lasting connections with our audience.

Inspired by these success stories, we created our legacy of impactful partnerships. Our initiatives were designed not just to enhance visibility but to enrich the lives of our customers, providing them with experiences and value that transcended the ordinary.

As we reflect on these journeys of collaboration and growth, it becomes clear that the essence of reciprocal marketing lies in its ability to foster genuine connections. It's a reminder that in the business world, the most enduring successes are those built on mutual respect, shared values, and the relentless pursuit of creating meaningful experiences.

The lessons gleaned from these examples continue to illuminate our path, guiding us toward a future where business is not just a transaction but a shared journey of growth, innovation, and community. As we move forward, armed with the insights and inspirations from those who have navigated this path before us, we remain committed to exploring new horizons of reciprocal marketing, always to create value that echoes far beyond the confines of our own ventures.

## Conclusion and Action Steps

Reflecting on our journey through reciprocal marketing, we've navigated from the foundational principles to the implementation and measurement of its impact, culminating in celebrating its successes through real-world examples. Each step has been a testament to the transformative power of building genuine relationships with our customers and partners.

As we stand at the precipice of this chapter's conclusion, it's essential to distill the essence of our exploration into actionable steps. This isn't just a narrative of past achievements but a blueprint for future endeavors. The heart of reciprocal marketing lies in its ability to forge connections that transcend the transactional, fostering a community built on mutual respect, shared values, and collective growth.

Here are five key actions to carry forward:

1. **Embrace a Giving Mindset:** Approach every customer interaction with the intent to provide value. This means thinking beyond immediate gains and considering how to positively impact your audience's lives.

2. **Forge Meaningful Partnerships:** Seek collaborations with businesses and individuals who share your ethos. These partnerships should amplify your reach and enrich the experience you offer your customers.

3. **Listen and Adapt:** Use feedback and data to refine your approach continually. The most successful reciprocal marketing strategies evolve in response to customer needs and market dynamics.

4. **Create Experiences:** Move beyond traditional marketing tactics by crafting experiences that resonate with your audience. Whether through events, content, or innovative services, aim to leave a lasting impression.

5. **Celebrate and Share Success:** Don't keep your victories to yourself. Share your successes and learnings with your community, fostering an environment of openness and mutual growth.

As we conclude this chapter, I invite you to join me on this ongoing journey of reciprocal marketing. Together, we can redefine the business landscape, building enterprises that thrive and contribute to the greater good. It's a path of endless discovery, challenge, and satisfaction. Let's embark on this adventure with the knowledge that the most enduring success comes from the value we create for others.

In the words of a journey we've shared, the power of reciprocity in marketing is not just a strategy but a philosophy—a way of doing business that elevates everyone involved. As we move forward, let us carry the torch of this philosophy high, lighting the way for a future where business is synonymous with generosity, collaboration, and mutual success.

# 10

# Creating a Culture of Mutual Respect and Appreciation

IN MY JOURNEY THROUGH the corporate world, navigating the complexities of leadership within a dental office's vibrant tapestry, I've realized the profound impact of cultivating a culture rooted in mutual respect and appreciation. This realization didn't dawn on me overnight. It was a lesson learned through the intricate dance of successes and setbacks, much like the stories shared in Daniel Coyle's "The Culture Code," a book that delves into the essence of successful group dynamics.

My story begins with a flashback to a particularly challenging period in our dental practice. We grappled with the all-too-common issue of siloed communication and disjointed team efforts, which invariably led to operational inefficiencies and palpable tension. During this time, an incident occurred, a moment that would become a turning point in how I viewed leadership and team dynamics.

One of our dental assistants, Sarah, suggested a new

patient scheduling system that promised to streamline our operations and improve patient experience. Initially, I was skeptical. After all, what could a dental assistant know about complex scheduling software? But her earnestness and thoughtful presentation of her case caught me off guard. This foreshadowed the untapped potential within our team, which could only be realized through a culture of respect and openness to every team member's contributions.

I decided to leap of faith and encourage Sarah to lead a pilot project implementing her suggested system. This decision sparked a series of dialogues within the team, opening up avenues for communication that had previously been barricaded by hierarchical mindsets. Through these conversations, a transformation began to unfold. The team started to see themselves as individuals performing their respective duties and as integral parts of a cohesive whole, contributing to a shared vision.

As the project took shape, the benefits of fostering an environment where every voice is heard and valued became increasingly evident. Not only did the new scheduling system prove to be a resounding success, streamlining our operations beyond our expectations, but the process also ignited a wave of innovation within the team. Ideas that had been dormant under the weight of a rigid corporate culture began to surface, driving improvements in our practice.

This experience taught me a crucial lesson about the power of mutual respect and appreciation in unlocking a team's potential. It highlighted the importance of creating a space where individuals feel safe sharing their ideas, where feedback is given and received with grace, and where each team member's contributions are recognized and celebrated.

Reflecting on this journey, I am reminded of the scenes in "The Culture Code," where Coyle emphasizes the significance of vulnerability, safety, and purpose in building strong, cohesive teams. My journey echoes the narratives in the book, underscoring the undeniable link between a culture of respect and the capacity for collective innovation and growth.

As I narrate this chapter of my story, it's with the understanding that creating a culture of mutual respect and appreciation is not a destination but a continuous journey. It requires constant nurturing, a commitment to personal growth, and an unwavering belief in the potential of people to rise above their perceived limitations when they are supported and valued.

This chapter will explore the transformative power of respect and appreciation in the workplace, sharing strategies for building this culture, methods to show appreciation effectively, and real-world examples of companies that have successfully embodied these values. I hope that through this exploration, you will find inspiration and practical guidance to cultivate a thriving, respectful, and appreciative culture within your own organizations, unlocking the door to unprecedented innovation and success.

## The Importance of Respect in the Workplace - Its role in creating a positive culture.

Navigating the corridors of our dental practice, the essence of respect in the workplace began to crystallize in my mind as the cornerstone of our collective journey toward innovation and excellence. Reflecting upon the incident with Sarah and her idea's transformative power to our operations, it dawned on me that this was merely a single thread in the rich tapestry of a respectful workplace culture.

I learned that respect was not just about acknowledging contributions or listening to suggestions; it was about creating an environment where every team member felt seen, heard, and valued. It was about dismantling the hierarchies that stifled creativity and replacing them with a culture of inclusivity where the janitor had as much voice as the senior dentist. This realization was a beacon, guiding me through the murky waters of leadership and toward a destination I had once thought unreachable.

In cultivating this culture, dialogue became our most powerful tool. We encouraged conversations that transcended professional boundaries, fostering community within our practice. These dialogues often revealed the diverse perspectives and unique insights each team member brought to the table, enriching our understanding and approach to challenges.

Moreover, this culture of respect manifests in our daily

interactions. Simple gestures of acknowledgment, whether through a morning greeting or a thank-you note for a job well done, became the norm rather than the exception. These acts, though small, were powerful affirmations of each person's value to our team.

The impact was palpable as our practice embraced this culture of mutual respect and appreciation. Team morale soared, and with it, productivity and innovation. We began to see decreased staff turnover, a testament to the positive work environment we had nurtured. Patients, too, noticed the change. They commented on the warmth and professionalism of our staff, aspects that contributed significantly to their overall satisfaction.

This journey of creating a culture of respect and appreciation taught me invaluable lessons about leadership and the power of collective effort. It underscored that a respectful workplace is a moral imperative and a strategic advantage. It is the soil where the seeds of innovation, commitment, and excellence are sown and nurtured.

As we progress in this chapter, I will share the strategies we employed to build this culture, the challenges we faced, and how we overcame them. I will delve into the methods of showing appreciation that resonate most deeply and explore the tangible benefits of a respectful and appreciative workplace culture. Through this narrative, I hope to offer insights and inspiration for leaders looking to cultivate a similar environment in their organizations, where respect and appreciation are ideals and lived realities.

## Strategies for Building Respect - How leaders can cultivate a respectful environment.

Building on the foundation of mutual respect and appreciation, the next step in our journey was to develop and implement strategies that would embed these values into the very fabric of our dental practice. This was no small feat. It required a deliberate shift in mindset from the top down and a commitment to consistent action to bring our vision to life.

Leading by example became my mantra. As the manager, I understood that the culture of our practice reflected my actions and attitudes. I made a concerted effort to demonstrate respect in all my interactions, whether with the newest hire or the most experienced dentist. This included actively listening to concerns, offering constructive feedback, and publicly acknowledging contributions, big or small.

Creating open lines of communication was another cornerstone of our strategy. We established regular team meetings as a forum for discussing operational issues and as a space for sharing ideas, concerns, and successes. These meetings were structured to ensure that everyone had a voice, and we utilized techniques like round-robin to ensure that each team member could share their thoughts without fear of judgment or reprisal.

In these sessions, we often revisited the principles shared in "The Culture Code" by Daniel Coyle, discussing how vulnerability, safety, and purpose played out in our own practice. These conversations were sometimes uncomfortable, as they challenged us to confront biases and assumptions that had gone unexamined. Yet, through this discomfort, we grew closer as a team, building a level of trust and understanding that became the bedrock of our culture.

Recognizing and celebrating achievements was another pivotal aspect of our strategy. We implemented a "kudos" board in the staff room where team members could post notes of appreciation for their colleagues. This simple initiative had a profound effect, creating a visible reminder of each person's value to our team. It also sparked a ripple effect, encouraging more spontaneous recognition and gratitude throughout the practice.

However, building a culture of respect and appreciation is not a one-and-done effort; it requires ongoing attention and adaptation. We learned to be agile, taking feedback from team members about what was working and what wasn't and adjusting our strategies accordingly. This iterative process was essential in ensuring that our culture remained vibrant and responsive to our team's needs.

Reflecting on this phase of our journey, I am struck by the transformative power of intentional leadership and collective commitment. By prioritizing respect and appreciation, we were able to enhance our workplace culture and drive tangible improvements in our operational efficiency and patient satisfaction. This chapter of our story is a testament to the idea that the heart of any successful organization lies in the strength of its relationships and that cultivating a culture of mutual respect and appreciation is perhaps the most impactful investment a leader can make.

## Appreciation as a Tool for Empowerment - Methods to show appreciation and its benefits.

Appreciation within the workplace has been a beacon, guiding our journey toward a culture where every individual feels valued and empowered. As we embarked on this path, I discovered the transformative power of expressing gratitude and recognition in diverse and meaningful ways.

In our practice, appreciation transcended mere acknowledgments. It became a vehicle for empowerment, a means to uplift and inspire every team member. We initiated a tradition of monthly appreciation meetings, a forum where achievements, no matter how small, were celebrated. This ritual fostered a sense of accomplishment and nurtured a culture of mutual respect and admiration.

Moreover, we introduced peer recognition programs that allowed team members to highlight the contributions of their colleagues. This peer-to-peer acknowledgment highlighted the often-overlooked acts of support, collaboration, and kindness that knit our team closer together. It underscored that appreciation is not solely the domain of leadership but a shared responsibility that enhances our collective sense of belonging and community.

Personalized gestures of gratitude also became a cornerstone of our appreciation strategy. Understanding that appreciation resonates differently with each individual, we endeavored to tailor our gestures to match our team members' unique preferences and aspirations. For some, it was the opportunity for professional development; for others, a handwritten note of thanks or public acknowledgment made all the difference. These personalized efforts did not go unnoticed. They were powerful affirmations of each individual's value to our team and practice.

The impact of these strategies was profound. Engagement and morale soared as team members felt genuinely recognized and valued. This heightened sense of belonging and appreciation translated into an unparalleled dedication to our mission and an unwavering commitment to excellence in patient care.

But the journey of cultivating a culture of appreciation taught me more than the mechanics of expressing gratitude. It revealed the deep-seated need for connection and recognition at every individual's heart. It reminded me that at the core of every thriving organization is acknowledging the human element, the understanding that beyond the roles and responsibilities lies a person whose contributions are worthy of recognition and respect.

As we continue to navigate the challenges and triumphs of our profession, the lessons learned from fostering a culture of appreciation remain a guiding light. They remind us that the strength of our practice lies not just in the skills and knowledge we possess but in the mutual respect, appreciation, and empowerment that bind us together. This journey of appreciation is a testament to the enduring power of gratitude in transforming not only our workplace but also the lives of those we touch through our work.

## Case Studies - Companies that have successfully built cultures of respect and appreciation.

Inspired by the success stories of Salesforce, Google, and Zappos, our dental practice embarked on a mission to weave a fabric of respect and appreciation deeply into our organizational culture. These companies, each a titan in its own right, demonstrated that the heart of their success lay not in the brilliance of their innovations alone but in the strength of their workplace culture. In this culture, every employee felt seen, heard, and valued.

Drawing from Salesforce's ethos of 'Ohana,' we sought to create an environment that mirrored a family-like support system. The notion that everyone—from dental hygienists to office managers—plays a vital role in our collective success became our guiding principle. This approach broke down barriers, fostering a sense of belonging and unity that propelled us toward shared goals with renewed vigor.

Similarly, Google's 'gPause' initiative inspired us to prioritize our team's well-being. Recognizing the importance of mental health and work-life balance, we introduced practices to reduce burnout and promote mindfulness. This improved our team's overall satisfaction and led to a noticeable uptick in creativity and productivity, proving that a well-rested mind is a fertile ground for innovation.

Zappos's unparalleled customer service and employee engagement offered yet another beacon. Emulating their model, we strongly emphasized internal recognition and empowerment, celebrating achievements and encouraging open dialogue. This fostered a culture where feedback was not just welcomed but actively sought, driving continuous improvement and a sense of ownership across all levels of our practice.

The journey was transformative. As we implemented these strategies, our practice began to evolve. The atmosphere of mutual respect and appreciation led to a cascade of positive outcomes: increased job satisfaction, lower turnover rates, and a significant enhancement in patient care and satisfaction. Our team, once siloed by departmental divides, now thrived as a cohesive unit, united by a common purpose and mutual respect.

Much like the narratives of Salesforce, Google, and Zappos,

this chapter of our story illustrates the profound impact of a workplace culture founded on respect and appreciation. It underscores the reality that such a culture is not a lofty ideal but a tangible, achievable state that yields not only enhanced performance and satisfaction but also a sense of fulfillment and purpose for everyone involved.

As I reflect on this journey, I'm filled with gratitude for the lessons learned and the growth experienced, both personally and collectively. The path to cultivating a culture of mutual respect and appreciation is ongoing, each step revealing new insights and opportunities for enrichment. It's a path we walk together, guided by the conviction that we unlock the full potential of our collective spirit and purpose in valuing each team member.

## Conclusion and Action Steps

Reflecting on our journey to create a culture of mutual respect and appreciation within our dental practice, it's clear that the transformations we've experienced are not just operational improvements but a fundamental shift in how we connect as a team and serve our community. This narrative, inspired by pioneers like Salesforce, Google, and Zappos and guided by insights from "The Culture Code," has shown us that the ethos of respect and appreciation is the backbone of enduring success and innovation.

As we draw this chapter to a close, the action steps forward are clear and are designed to ensure that the culture of mutual respect and appreciation continues to flourish:

1. **Continue Leading by Example:** As leaders, our behavior sets the tone. Commit to demonstrating respect and appreciation daily.

2. **Maintain Open Lines of Communication:** Foster an environment where team members feel comfortable sharing ideas and feedback.

3. **Regular Recognition:** Implement regular opportunities to recognize and celebrate the contributions of all team members and acknowledge their value to the team.

4. **Personalize Appreciation:** Understand and respect each team member's individuality, tailoring appreciation to their unique preferences and contributions.

5. **Foster Continuous Learning:** Encourage a culture of growth and development, emphasizing the role of respect and appreciation in fostering a positive learning environment.

These steps are not the end but a continuation of our commitment to cultivating a workplace where everyone feels respected, valued, and empowered to contribute their best.

Through mutual respect and appreciation, we enhance our workplace and set a standard for excellence that resonates throughout our community and beyond.

Building and maintaining a culture of respect and appreciation requires vigilance, dedication, and an open heart. It's a path that promises improved operational efficiency, team morale, and a deeper sense of connection and purpose. As we move forward, let's carry the lessons of this chapter with us, embracing each day as an opportunity to strengthen the bonds that unite us and to create a legacy of respect and appreciation that endures for generations to come.

# 11

# The Art of Ethical Persuasion in Sales

I N MY EARLY DAYS of navigating the bustling business world, I came across a gem of a book, "To Sell Is Human" by Daniel H. Pink, that fundamentally altered my perspective on sales. It wasn't just a book; it was a revelation that selling, at its core, isn't about convincing someone to part with their money. It's about moving others, ethically and effectively, to align with a vision or solution that benefits all involved. This insight didn't just change my approach to business; it revolutionized it.

I remember a time when this philosophy was put to the test. It was during my tenure as a leader in a company that prided itself on not just the quality of our products but on the values we upheld in every transaction. My colleague, Alex, had recently ventured into sales, moving from our team to spearhead the outreach for our new line of eco-friendly cleaning products. His first significant opportunity came with Sarah, the owner of a quaint boutique hotel known for its commitment to sustainability.

Alex's approach was nothing short of what I'd call ethical persuasion. He did his homework, learning about Sarah's hotel and her dedication to reducing environmental impact. When they met, Alex's pitch was not about selling a product but about offering a solution that resonated deeply with Sarah's values and her hotel's mission. Sure, he talked about the benefits of our eco-friendly cleaning products, but he went further. Alex truly listened to Sarah's concerns and tailored his suggestions to fit her unique needs.

This wasn't a one-off meeting with a sales agenda; it was the beginning of a partnership based on mutual respect and shared goals. Alex offered Sarah a trial period to experience the products without strings attached. This gesture of good faith paid off. The products proved their worth, and the ethical approach Alex took built a foundation of trust and respect between our company and Sarah's hotel.

The success of this partnership taught me a valuable lesson: ethical persuasion in sales is about more than just transactions. It's about creating relationships built on trust, understanding, and shared values. It's a long-term investment in the well-being of your customers and, by extension, your business.

Reflecting on this journey, I'm reminded of the importance of integrating ethical persuasion into all aspects of our business practices. It's not just a sales technique; it's a philosophy that guides how we interact with everyone, from our customers to our colleagues. Ethical persuasion is rooted in authenticity, respect, and a genuine desire to contribute positively to the lives of those we touch through our work.

In this chapter, we'll explore the art of ethical persuasion in sales, drawing on real-world examples and personal experiences to illuminate how it can transform business relationships and outcomes. We'll delve into understanding ethical persuasion, distinguishing it from manipulation, and showcasing its long-term benefits for businesses and customers. Along the way, I'll share strategies and techniques for ethically persuading others, grounded in respect, transparency, and a deep commitment to serving the genuine needs of our customers.

Join me as we journey through this exploration of ethical persuasion. This path promises business success and a more meaningful and impactful way of engaging with the world around us. Through this exploration, we'll discover that at the heart of every successful transaction lies the potential for positive change for our businesses, customers, and communities. This is the promise of ethical persuasion in sales, which guides us toward a future where business is not just about profit but purpose.

So, let's embark on this journey together, drawing inspiration from the principles of reciprocity, the power of ethical persuasion, and the transformative potential of conducting business with a conscience. This path has not only shaped my career but has also illuminated the way forward for those of us who dare to envision a business landscape defined by integrity, sustainability, and shared success.

## Understanding Ethical Persuasion - Defining and Differentiating it from Manipulation

As we delve deeper into the art of ethical persuasion in sales, it's crucial to understand its essence. Ethical persuasion is not about manipulation or coercion; it's about influencing others through honesty, integrity, and genuine care for their needs and values. It's a subtle dance between expressing your message and listening intently to the other person, ensuring that any action taken is mutually beneficial. This approach is morally right and incredibly effective in building lasting business relationships.

One of the key distinctions of ethical persuasion lies in its foundation: respect and appreciation. I've seen firsthand how companies that foster a culture of respect thrive internally and excel in customer interactions. Salesforce, for example, is renowned for its commitment to inclusivity and ethical practices. They've created an environment where employees feel valued, reflecting how they treat customers. Similarly, Google's initiatives like "pause" and Zappos' focus on exceptional customer service are a testament to the power of respect in the workplace and the marketplace. These companies understand that ethical persuasion starts with how they treat their people.

Understanding ethical persuasion also means recognizing what it's not. It's not about pushing your agenda or prioritizing your needs over those of your customers. It's about finding that sweet spot where your offerings align perfectly with your customer's needs, even if it means recommending a solution you don't provide. This level of honesty and transparency sets apart true ethical persuasion from mere sales tactics.

I learned the importance of this distinction early in my career. A turning point was a meeting with a potential client, where instead of pushing our newest product, we discussed their actual needs. It became clear that what they needed most wasn't what we were there to sell. We built a relationship based on trust by acknowledging this and helping them find the right solution—even though it wasn't ours. This client became one of our most loyal customers, not because we sold them something, but because we helped them solve a problem. This experience taught me that ethical persuasion is about adding real value, not just making a sale.

This approach requires a deep understanding of your customers. It's about listening more than you talk, asking the right questions, and genuinely caring about the answers. It's about empathy—putting yourself in their shoes to understand their challenges and aspirations. When you approach sales from this perspective, you're not just a vendor but a trusted advisor.

In my journey, I've adopted several techniques to practice ethical persuasion effectively:

> 1. Active Listening: Truly listening to what the customer says (and doesn't say) is the first step in understanding their needs. It's not about waiting for your turn to speak; it's about hearing to understand and respond

thoughtfully.

2. Honest Communication: Always be truthful about what your product can and cannot do. Honesty builds trust, and trust is the foundation of any lasting relationship.

3. Tailored Solutions: No two customers are the same. Tailor your approach based on each customer's specific needs and concerns, showing that you see them as individuals.

4. Long-term Thinking: Focus on building a lasting relationship, not just closing a sale. When customers feel valued, they're more likely to become loyal advocates for your brand.

5. Adding Value Beyond the Sale: Offer insights, advice, or resources that can help the customer, even if it doesn't lead to an immediate sale. This generosity demonstrates your commitment to their success.

Sharing these insights reminds me of the stories of companies like Salesforce, Google, and Zappos. They've built cultures that embody ethical persuasion, resulting in unparalleled customer loyalty and brand strength. These examples inspire me to strive for excellence in every interaction, ensuring that my actions always align with the principles of ethical persuasion.

In the next sections, we'll explore ethical persuasion techniques in more detail, highlighting how to apply these principles in your sales strategy. We'll also examine the long-term benefits of this approach, proving that ethical persuasion is not just good practice—it's good business. Through real-life examples and practical advice, I hope to inspire you to embrace ethical persuasion as a cornerstone of your sales philosophy, transforming how you connect with customers and grow your business.

## Techniques of Ethical Persuasion - How to persuade ethically in sales.

Diving into the heart of ethical persuasion in sales, dissecting the techniques that embolden this approach, and transforming every interaction into an opportunity for genuine connection and mutual growth are paramount. The essence of ethical persuasion lies in aligning your product or service with your customer's needs and values, forging a pathway toward not just a sale but a relationship steeped in trust and mutual respect.

One foundational technique of ethical persuasion is the art of building trust. Trust is not given lightly; it's earned through consistent, transparent, and honest communication. In every interaction with potential clients, I make it my mission to present our offerings transparently, highlighting the strengths and limitations. This honesty might seem counterintuitive in a sales context, where the aim is to impress. However, I've found that this vulnerability breeds trust, a crucial ingredient for lasting business relationships.

Transparency extends beyond the features of a product or service. It encompasses the entire ethos of your company. For instance, if a customer is concerned about environmental impact, sharing your company's sustainability practices can reinforce the alignment of your values with theirs. This alignment is not just persuasive; it's compelling because it speaks to something greater than the transaction—it speaks to shared goals and values.

Another pivotal technique is tailored communication. No two customers are the same, and their needs can be vastly different. Ethical persuasion requires a deep understanding of these needs, achieved through active listening and empathy. When I prepare for a sales meeting, I spend more time researching the client's background, challenges, and aspirations than rehearsing my pitch. This preparation allows me to tailor my communication, ensuring I'm addressing their specific concerns and how our offerings can provide value to them.

Persuasion, in its ethical form, also involves guiding the customer through the decision-making process with integrity. It's about being a consultant rather than a salesperson. I often find myself discussing various options with customers, even those my company doesn't offer. This approach might seem like a sales deterrent, but it cements our credibility and often leads the customer back to us, convinced by our commitment to their best interest.

Moreover, ethical persuasion is characterized by a focus on long-term relationships over immediate gains. This long-term vision involves regular follow-ups, offering continued support, and checking in on the customer's satisfaction with the product or service. It's about ensuring they feel valued and supported long after the sale. This dedication to customer satisfaction nurtures a loyalty that transcends transactional interactions, transforming customers into advocates for your brand.

Lastly, ethical persuasion involves continuous learning and adaptation. The landscape of customer needs and values is ever-evolving, and staying attuned to these changes is crucial. I make it a point to gather feedback, engage in conversations, and stay informed about industry trends. This commitment to growth improves our offerings and demonstrates to customers that we are invested in continually providing value.

Through these techniques, ethical persuasion becomes more than a sales strategy; it becomes a philosophy that guides every interaction. This is a testament to the belief that business success is not measured solely by profit margins but by our positive impact on our customers and the world around us.

In my journey, I've witnessed the transformative power of ethical persuasion. It has led to successful sales and fostered enduring relationships built on mutual trust and respect. As we move forward, I'm eager to delve deeper into the long-term benefits of this approach, illustrating why ethical persuasion is not merely a choice but a necessity for sustainable business success. Join me as we explore the enduring impact of conducting business with integrity, empathy, and a genuine commitment to the well-being of our customers.

## The Long-Term Benefits - Why ethical persuasion is beneficial in the long run.

Venturing further into ethical persuasion, it's vital to illuminate the long-term benefits that extend far beyond the immediacy of a successful sale. This approach to business is not just a strategy; it's a philosophy that shapes every facet of your operations, nurturing a culture of trust, respect, and mutual benefit that stands the test of time.

One of the most profound benefits of ethical persuasion is cultivating trust. In a world brimming with skepticism towards sales and marketing tactics, earning the trust of your customers is invaluable. This trust is not merely about believing in the quality of your products or services; it's about faith in your integrity as a business. When customers know that you prioritize their needs and values, even at the cost of a short-term sale, you're not just making a customer for a day but likely securing a loyal advocate for life.

Trust naturally leads to the development of long-lasting relationships. These relationships are the cornerstone of any successful business, especially in industries where repeat business and referrals are paramount. Ethical persuasion ensures that your interactions are not transactional but transformational, fostering a deep connection between your brand and your customers. It's about creating a narrative of shared success, where your growth is directly tied to your positive impact on the lives of those you serve.

Furthermore, ethical persuasion plays a critical role in brand reputation. In the digital age, a company's reputation can be its most valuable asset or its greatest liability. By embracing ethical persuasion, you're not just avoiding the pitfalls of negative reviews or bad press but actively building a positive narrative around your brand. Customers are more inclined to share their positive experiences when they feel genuinely cared for and valued. This word-of-mouth marketing is incredibly powerful, as it comes with authenticity and credibility that traditional advertising can't match.

Another significant benefit is the enhancement of employee morale and engagement. When your team sees that your business practices align with ethical standards and that you're building genuine relationships with customers, it instills a sense of pride and purpose in their work. Employees are more motivated when they know they're contributing to something meaningful beyond hitting sales targets. This sense of purpose can lead to higher productivity, lower turnover rates, and an overall positive workplace culture that attracts top talent.

Ethical persuasion also mitigates risk. In an era where consumers are increasingly aware and vocal about their expectations for corporate responsibility, businesses that fail to act ethically are at risk of public backlash, legal troubles, and financial losses. Ethical persuasion, by its nature, requires a commitment to transparency, honesty, and respect, which can protect your business from potential pitfalls associated with deceptive or aggressive sales tactics.

Lastly, ethical persuasion aligns with the growing consumer demand for businesses that contribute positively to society. Today's consumers are not just buying products or services but buying into what a brand stands for. By embedding ethical persuasion into your business practices, you're positioning your brand as one that not only meets the immediate needs of its customers but also contributes to the greater good. This alignment with consumer values can be a significant differentiator in crowded markets, offering a competitive edge that is both sustainable and impactful.

As I reflect on the journey of embedding ethical persuasion into my business practices, I'm reminded of the countless stories of customers who became more like partners, of employees who became ambassadors of our brand, and of a community that grew to trust and support us not just for what we sell but for who we are. This journey has shown me that the true measure of success is not in quarterly profits but in our lasting impact on the lives of those we touch through our work.

In the next section, we will explore real-life examples of businesses that have thrived by embracing ethical persuasion, showcasing the tangible benefits of this approach. These stories will serve as inspiration and a testament to the transformative power of conducting business with a conscience. Join me as we explore the path of ethical persuasion, a journey that promises business success and a legacy of positive impact and enduring relationships.

## Real-Life Examples - Success stories of businesses that use ethical persuasion effectively.

As we journey through the landscape of ethical persuasion, the tales of businesses that have flourished by embracing this philosophy are both inspiring and instructive. These real-life examples serve as beacons, illuminating the path for others to follow and showcasing the tangible benefits of building a business based on integrity, empathy, and genuine customer care.

One such paragon of ethical persuasion is Patagonia, the outdoor clothing and gear company. Patagonia's ethos is deeply rooted in environmental sustainability and ethical business practices, which resonate profoundly with its customer base. Their approach to sales is less about persuasion and more about education, focusing on informing customers about the environmental impact of their purchases and encouraging them to make more conscious choices. Patagonia's "Worn Wear" program exemplifies this, inviting customers to repair their gear rather than buy new, embodying the principle of reducing consumption for the planet's sake. This commitment to ethical practices has garnered Patagonia a loyal following and positioned the brand as a leader in corporate responsibility, proving that ethical persuasion can drive both brand loyalty and commercial success.

Another example is the tech giant Salesforce. Salesforce has built its reputation on more than just innovative products; it's known for its commitment to ethical practices, community engagement, and inclusive culture. Salesforce's 1-1-1 model of philanthropy, dedicating 1% of its product, equity, and employee time to community initiatives, demonstrates a genuine commitment to giving back. This ethos of care and responsibility permeates every aspect of Salesforce's operations, including sales, where transparency and customer success are paramount. Salesforce's approach to ethical persuasion, prioritizing customer needs and societal impact, has led to remarkable business growth and established the company as a model of corporate citizenship.

Zappos, the online shoe and clothing retailer, stands out for its unparalleled customer service, a cornerstone of its business model. Zappos' success is built on the belief that happy customers are the key to a profitable business. This belief is reflected in their sales approach, which emphasizes customer satisfaction. Zappos' 365-day return policy and free shipping are a testament to their commitment to making the shopping experience as easy and risk-free as possible for their customers. By prioritizing customer happiness through ethical persuasion and service, Zappos has achieved extraordinary customer loyalty and retention rates, showcasing the power of putting customer needs at the heart of business decisions.

These stories exemplify the essence of ethical persuasion and its profound impact on building successful, sustainable businesses. Patagonia, Salesforce, and Zappos are a few examples of companies operating on principles of integrity, transparency, and genuine care for their customers and communities. Their success stories serve as compelling evidence that ethical persuasion is not just a moral choice but a strategic one that leads to lasting growth, brand loyalty, and a positive corporate legacy.

Reflecting on my journey, I am inspired by these examples to continue championing ethical persuasion in every aspect of my business. It reaffirms my belief that success achieved through ethical means is more rewarding and sustainable in the long run. As we forge ahead, let us carry the lessons learned from these trailblazers, embracing ethical persuasion not just as a sales strategy but as a guiding principle for conducting business. In doing so, we can aspire not only to achieve our business goals but also to positively impact the world around us, one ethical decision at a time.

As we conclude this exploration of ethical persuasion, remember that the journey does not end here. It's a continuous learning process, a process of growing and striving to align our business practices with our core values. Let us move forward with the conviction that through ethical persuasion, we can transform not just our businesses but also the lives of our customers, our communities, and, ultimately, the world.

## Conclusion and Action Steps

As we draw this chapter to a close, it's important to pause and reflect on our journey together. We've explored the vast and vibrant terrain of ethical persuasion in sales, a landscape where integrity, empathy, and genuine care for the customer are not just ethical choices but strategic ones that lead to sustainable business success. This journey has been about more than just improving sales tactics; it's been about transforming our business ethos.

As we've seen through examples like Patagonia, Salesforce, and Zappos, ethical persuasion is a powerful tool for building lasting relationships, fostering brand loyalty, and driving growth. These companies have shown us that when businesses operate with a genuine commitment to their customer's needs and values, they succeed commercially and contribute positively to society.

But how do we translate these insights into actionable steps for our businesses? How do we ensure that ethical persuasion becomes ingrained in our sales approach, customer interactions, and corporate culture?

The first step is to embrace transparency. This means being open about our products and services, including their benefits and limitations. It's about ensuring that our customers have all the information they need to make informed decisions, even if it means recommending a solution we don't offer. Transparency builds trust, and trust is the cornerstone of any lasting relationship.

Second, we must prioritize active listening and empathy. This involves truly understanding our customers' needs, challenges, and aspirations. By putting ourselves in their shoes, we can tailor our solutions to provide genuine value, deepen the connection, and foster loyalty.

Third, we should focus on long-term relationships rather than short-term gains. This means following up with customers, offering continued support, and demonstrating that we value their business for the sale and the ongoing relationship. Such a commitment to customer satisfaction ensures that our business is built on trust and mutual respect.

Fourth, we need to embed ethical persuasion into our corporate culture. This requires training our teams on the importance of ethics in sales and customer interactions, encouraging a mindset that values long-term relationships over immediate transactions. When our entire team operates with integrity and empathy, our business becomes a living testament to the power of ethical persuasion.

Finally, continuous improvement and adaptation are crucial. Our customers' needs and values evolve, and so should our approach to ethical persuasion. By staying attuned to these changes and being willing to adjust our strategies accordingly, we ensure that our business remains relevant and responsive to the market.

Implementing these steps improves our sales outcomes and elevates our business as a whole. We become a brand that customers trust, advocate for, and remain loyal to over time. We build a business that not only achieves financial success but also positively impacts the world.

As we conclude this chapter, I invite you to join me on this journey of ethical persuasion. Let us apply the insights and strategies we've discussed and apply them to our businesses, customer interactions, and personal lives. Let us strive to be leaders who achieve success, inspire change, build profitable businesses, and contribute to a better world.

Remember, the journey of ethical persuasion is ongoing. It's a path marked by continuous learning, growth, and a steadfast commitment to doing what's right. By walking this path, we can transform our businesses, enrich the lives of our customers, and leave a lasting legacy of positive impact.

Let's take the first step today, inspired by the examples we've explored and motivated by the promise of what we can achieve together. Through ethical persuasion, we can build businesses that are not only successful but also meaningful, businesses that stand as pillars of integrity, empathy, and genuine care in the marketplace.

Thank you for joining me on this journey. Together, let's pave the way for a future where business is synonymous with ethical persuasion, where success is measured not just by profit but by our positive impact on the world.

# 12

# Leveraging Reciprocity for Sustainable Business Growth

A s I SIT DOWN to pen this chapter, my thoughts drift to the countless interactions and decisions that have shaped my journey in the business world. Each one is a testament to the profound power of reciprocity, not just as a principle but as a transformative force capable of propelling businesses to new heights. It's a realization I came to, much like many before me, not through abstract theories but through tangible, lived experiences. This chapter, dear reader, invites you to explore the untapped potential of leveraging reciprocity for sustainable business growth.

Reflecting on the wisdom imparted in "To Sell Is Human" by Daniel H. Pink, I'm reminded that sales aren't about manipulation or coercion; it's about moving others, ethically and authentically. Pink's insights into the art of selling resonate deeply with me, especially his emphasis on the human element—on empathy, clarity, and the service we provide to others. It's a perspective that has influenced how I approach sales and envision the broader scope of business strategy and growth.

Allow me to share a story that epitomizes ethical persuasion in action—a narrative I heard about a peer in the competitive landscape of healthcare technology. This colleague, let's call him John, was introduced to a clinic manager, whom we'll refer to as Dr. Lee, who is interested in innovative patient management systems but wary of data security issues. John, eschewing the aggressive pitch, opted for transparency and empathy. He discussed Dr. Lee's concerns, offering clear, detailed explanations of the security measures and the long-term benefits of the technology. John's aim wasn't just to secure a sale, build trust, and offer genuine value.

This approach didn't just win Dr. Lee over; it transformed him into a vocal advocate for the technology, leading to numerous referrals. This story beautifully illustrates the impact of ethical persuasion and its pivotal role in fostering lasting customer relationships. This experience was a powerful lesson in the importance of ethical persuasion and its role in building sustainable customer relationships.

As we delve into this chapter, I invite you to consider the broader implications of these principles for your business. We'll explore the concept of sustainability through reciprocity, a principle that champions mutual benefit and long-term growth over short-sighted gains. Companies like Patagonia have shown us that it's possible to thrive by putting ethical practices and environmental responsibility at the heart of their business model. Their commitment to transparency, product longevity, and environmental activism has garnered them a loyal customer base and driven substantial business success.

Our journey together in this chapter will also explore the critical importance of incorporating reciprocity into business strategies. This is about looking beyond the immediate transaction to creating lasting value for your customers, employees, and the community. It's about understanding that the most successful businesses give as much as they take.

We'll examine how businesses can adapt to change by embracing the principles of reciprocity. In a world where market conditions are constantly evolving, the ability to adapt and respond to the needs of your stakeholders can set you apart. Reciprocal businesses are uniquely positioned to navigate these changes, leveraging their strong relationships and collaborative networks to remain resilient and agile.

Finally, we will celebrate the success stories of businesses that have achieved sustainable growth through reciprocity. These companies have recognized that true success comes not from maximizing profits at all costs but from fostering a culture of giving, ethical persuasion, and building relationships that stand the test of time.

As we embark on this exploration, I encourage you to consider how the principles of reciprocity can be integrated into your business practices. How can you move beyond transactional interactions to build genuine, lasting relationships with your customers? How can you leverage the power of ethical persuasion to not only drive sales but also advocate for greater social and environmental responsibility?

This chapter is more than just a collection of insights and strategies; it's a roadmap to transforming your business through the power of reciprocity. It's about understanding that the most enduring path to growth and success benefits everyone it touches. So, let's dive in, together, into the heart of what it means to run a business that seeks to profit and make a meaningful impact in the world.

## Sustainability through Reciprocity - Linking reciprocal practices with sustainable growth.

Diving deeper into the heart of reciprocity, we find ourselves at the intersection of sustainability and business growth. This juncture is crucial, representing a fundamental shift in how businesses perceive their role in society and the environment. One cannot talk about this shift without mentioning Patagonia, a beacon of how reciprocal practices can lead to remarkable business success and sustainability.

Patagonia's journey is not just a story of a company selling outdoor gear; it's a narrative that redefines the very essence of business. Their unwavering commitment to environmental sustainability and ethical business practices has set a new benchmark for what it means to operate responsibly. Through transparent communication about their supply chain, advocacy for environmental causes, and a culture that encourages product repairs over replacements, they've done more than just sell; they've inspired a movement.

What strikes me the most about Patagonia is its genuine dedication to the principle of giving back, which resonates deeply with my beliefs. I remember learning about their "1% for the Planet" initiative, where they commit 1% of their total sales to environmental groups. It was a profound moment for me, illuminating how businesses could operate with a greater purpose beyond profit.

Patagonia's approach, rooted in ethical persuasion and reciprocal practices, has cultivated a fiercely loyal customer base. Customers are drawn not just to the quality of the products but also to the company's ethos. This is a powerful reminder that when businesses invest in building genuine relationships with their customers and communities, the return transcends the financial. It builds an invaluable legacy of trust and loyalty.

In my journey, I've strived to embody these principles within my own business. I've learned that sustainability through reciprocity is not just about environmental stewardship; it's about creating a business model that thrives on mutual benefit. This means engaging with our customers in a way that goes beyond the transactional, seeking to understand their needs and values and finding ways to meet them where they are.

For instance, we once organized a community event focusing on sustainable living practices. It wasn't directly related to our core business operations, but it was an issue close to our hearts and that of our customers. The event was a tremendous success, not just in turnout but in the depth of connections it fostered. It was a clear demonstration of reciprocity in action—by offering value to our community, we deepened our relationships with our customers, who, in turn, became more engaged and loyal advocates of our brand.

This experience taught me an invaluable lesson: giving and providing genuine value is a powerful form of persuasion. It's not about convincing someone to buy; it's about demonstrating your commitment to their well-being and the causes they care about. This, in turn, builds a bond of trust that is the foundation of a sustainable business.

As we navigate the complexities of today's business landscape, the principles of reciprocity and sustainability offer a beacon of hope. They remind us that success is not just measured by the bottom line, but by the positive impact, we can have on the world around us. It's a challenging path, no doubt, but one that is infinitely rewarding.

Incorporating these principles into your business strategy requires a shift in mindset. It calls for a focus on long-term relationships over short-term gains, genuine engagement with customers and communities, and commitment to operating ethically and sustainably. It's about viewing every decision through the lens of mutual benefit—how can we grow our business and contribute positively to our customers' lives and the world?

The journey of Patagonia has been a source of inspiration for me, as I'm sure it has been for many others. It is a powerful example of how businesses can achieve remarkable growth and sustainability by embracing reciprocity. As we move forward, let us carry this inspiration into our own practices, striving to create businesses that are not only successful but also purposeful and impactful.

This chapter focused on sustainability through reciprocity, is just the beginning. It's an invitation to rethink how we approach business, to challenge the status quo, and to embrace a model that values giving as much as receiving. As we delve into the subsequent sections, I'll share more insights and strategies for integrating these principles into your business for long-term success and impact. Together, let's embark on this journey of transformation driven by the power of reciprocity.

## Long-Term Planning - Incorporating reciprocity into business strategies for longevity.

In the world of business, where the terrain is ever-evolving and the stakes perennially high, the concept of reciprocity stands as a lighthouse, guiding towards a harbor of sustainable success and mutual prosperity. My journey, amid trials, triumphs, and transformations, has led me to embrace this principle as a strategy and a cornerstone of business ethos. In this section, we delve into the essence of long-term planning. In this venture, reciprocity is included and integrated into the fabric of business strategies for enduring longevity and resilience.

The realization that incorporating reciprocity into business strategies is pivotal for ensuring long-term success dawned on me during introspection and strategic realignment in my career. It was a period marked by the quest for a deeper meaning in business operations beyond mere profitability. This quest led to the understanding that businesses, at their core, are ecosystems of relationships—relationships with customers, partners, employees, and the community at large. Nurturing these relationships through reciprocity transforms them into robust pillars that support and sustain business growth over time.

Implementing reciprocity in business strategies requires a paradigm shift—a move from the conventional transactional mindset to a relational approach. This shift means prioritizing value creation for all stakeholders, not just shareholders. It's about seeing customers as partners in a shared journey, employees as co-creators of success, and the community as an extended family whose welfare is intertwined with the businesses. When this perspective becomes ingrained in the business model, every decision and action is evaluated not just on its immediate impact but on its contribution to building trust, enhancing relationships, and fostering a sense of mutual benefit.

I recall a significant turning point in our business when we decided to reevaluate our customer service strategy through the lens of reciprocity. Instead of viewing customer service as a cost center, we began to see it as an investment in building lasting relationships. We introduced initiatives that focused on genuinely understanding and addressing our customers' needs, even if it meant going beyond the standard protocols. This approach not only elevated customer satisfaction but also increased customer loyalty and referrals, demonstrating that when businesses give more in value than they take in payment, they set the stage for sustainable growth.

Moreover, incorporating reciprocity into our business strategy meant looking beyond the immediate business ecosystem to consider our impact on the broader community and environment. We initiated partnerships with local non-profits and embarked on sustainability projects, actions that not only contributed to societal and environmental well-being but also resonated deeply with our customers and employees, further strengthening our relationships with them.

However, integrating reciprocity into business strategies is not without its challenges. It requires patience, as the fruits of such endeavors may not be immediately visible. It demands a commitment to transparency and ethical conduct, ensuring that the pursuit of mutual benefit is genuine and not merely a marketing facade. It necessitates a culture of adaptability as the needs and expectations of stakeholders evolve over time.

Yet, the rewards of this approach are manifold and profound.

Businesses that embrace reciprocity as a strategic pillar discover that it enhances their reputation and brand loyalty and fosters innovation and resilience. In an age where consumers are increasingly looking to support businesses that align with their values, those who practice reciprocity find themselves at a competitive advantage.

As I reflect on the journey thus far, it's clear that integrating reciprocity into business strategies is not merely a choice but a necessity for those aiming for long-term success and sustainability. It's a commitment to operating in a way that enriches all stakeholders, creating a cycle of positive impact that fuels both business growth and societal progress.

In the following sections, we will explore further how businesses can adapt to change and navigate market shifts by adhering to the principles of reciprocity. We will also celebrate the success stories of businesses that have flourished by making reciprocity an integral part of their growth strategy. As we continue this exploration, I invite you to ponder how you can integrate these principles into your own business to grow and thrive in harmony with your community, environment, and values. Together, let's chart a course toward a future where business success is measured by financial performance and the positive impact we create in the world.

## Adapting to Change - How reciprocal businesses can effectively navigate market changes.

Navigating the choppy waters of the marketplace requires more than just a keen eye for trends and a knack for innovation. It demands a foundation built on principles that endure through seasons of change. Among these, reciprocity stands out as a compass guiding businesses toward surviving and thriving amidst market shifts. My journey, marked by ebbs and flows, has taught me the invaluable lesson that businesses rooted in reciprocal relationships are uniquely equipped to adapt and flourish.

The essence of reciprocal businesses lies in their foundational belief in mutual benefit. This core belief transforms how they interact with every stakeholder, from customers and employees to suppliers and the community. Such businesses understand that value creation is a two-way street, where listening and responding to the needs of stakeholders is paramount. This responsive nature enables reciprocal businesses to pivot and adapt with agility when faced with market changes.

Reflecting on my own experiences, I've seen firsthand how a reciprocal approach can foster a culture of openness and collaboration. We prioritized engaging in honest, open dialogues with our customers, seeking their feedback not just as a formality but as a crucial input into our decision-making process. This ongoing conversation helped us stay attuned to their evolving needs and preferences, allowing us to adapt our offerings in ways that truly resonated with them.

Moreover, this commitment to reciprocal relationships extended to our employees as well. By fostering a work environment that valued their insights and well-being, we cultivated a team that was highly motivated and deeply invested in the company's success. This investment translated into a flexible, innovative workforce ready to embrace change, turning potential disruptions into opportunities for growth.

Our approach to navigating market changes also involved collaborating with our business partners and suppliers. We viewed these relationships as not transactional contracts but strategic alliances, where shared success was the goal. This perspective ensured that when market shifts occurred, we could rely on a network of partners willing to work together to find solutions, whether by adapting supply chains, exploring new markets, or co-developing innovative products.

Adaptability, fueled by reciprocity, also meant being proactive about the broader impact of our business decisions. Recognizing that our actions reverberate within the community and the environment, we took steps to ensure that our responses to market changes were beneficial for the business and sustainable in the long term. This holistic view of business success — one that encompasses financial health, community well-being, and environmental stewardship — has been a key factor in our resilience and adaptability.

However, embracing reciprocity as a guiding principle in

navigating market changes is challenging. It requires a willingness to invest in relationships without guaranteeing immediate returns. It calls for a level of transparency and vulnerability that can be daunting. And it necessitates a culture that values long-term impact over short-term gains.

Yet, the rewards of this approach are unmistakable. Reciprocal businesses are often seen as more trustworthy and reliable by their stakeholders, which translates into stronger, more loyal relationships. These relationships become the bedrock upon which businesses can weather market volatility, emerging not just unscathed but stronger and more aligned with their stakeholders' needs and values.

As we move forward in this chapter, and as you, the reader, reflect on your business practices, I encourage you to consider how the principle of reciprocity can be woven into the fabric of your strategy. Think about how fostering mutual benefit can enhance your ability to adapt to change, how investing in relationships can build a resilient and agile business, and how prioritizing the well-being of all stakeholders can lead to sustainable, long-term success.

In the next section, we will celebrate the stories of businesses that have harnessed the power of reciprocity to achieve remarkable growth and resilience. These success stories serve as an inspiration and a testament to the transformative potential of reciprocity in business. Join me as we continue to explore the endless possibilities that unfold when we build our businesses on the foundation of giving, sharing, and mutual respect.

## Success Stories - Businesses that have achieved sustainable growth through reciprocity.

As I reflect on the journey thus far, the stories of success truly encapsulate the essence of what it means to embrace reciprocity in business. These narratives not only inspire but also serve as beacons of possibility for businesses aspiring to grow sustainably and ethically. Among these tales, one particularly resonates with me, not just for its success but also for the profound impact it has had on its community and industry.

Patagonia, synonymous with environmental sustainability and ethical business practices, stands out as a luminary in reciprocal business. Their story is not just about selling outdoor clothing and gear; it's a testament to the power of building a business by giving back and fostering mutual benefit. From the onset, Patagonia has been unwavering in its commitment to environmental activism, transparent communication, and creating high-quality products that last. But it's their dedication to the principle of reciprocity that truly sets them apart.

I remember my first encounter with Patagonia's ethos. Their "Don't Buy This Jacket" campaign caught my attention—a bold move that encouraged customers to reconsider the need for purchase in light of the environmental impact. This campaign, paradoxical as it may seem, was a profound act of reciprocity. Patagonia puts the planet's well-being and future generations above immediate profit. This approach heightened their brand loyalty and underscored the depth of their commitment to their values.

Drawing inspiration from Patagonia, I integrated similar practices within my business, focusing on long-term relationships with customers, sustainability, and ethical practices. We started small, with initiatives to reduce our environmental footprint and engage our customers in these efforts. Whether through sustainable sourcing or encouraging product longevity, each step was guided by the principle of reciprocity—giving back more than we take.

The journey wasn't without its hurdles. Shifting focus from short-term gains to long-term sustainability required not just a strategy change but a mindset transformation. Yet, the more we aligned our operations with the principles of reciprocity, the clearer the benefits became. Our customers appreciated the transparency and genuine commitment to ethical practices, which fostered a deeper loyalty and trust in our brand.

But Patagonia and my own experience are just two threads in a larger tapestry of success stories woven from the fabric of reciprocity. Across industries, businesses that have embraced this principle have found financial success and cultivated a sense of purpose and community. They've proven that it's possible to thrive by prioritizing the well-being of all stakeholders—customers, employees, communities, and the environment.

These success stories are not anomalies but evidence of a shifting paradigm in the business world. A shift towards recognizing that true success comes not from how much we can extract but from how much we can contribute. It's a realization that the most enduring and impactful businesses are those built on mutual benefit and respect.

As we stand on the brink of this paradigm shift, the question for each of us in the business world is not whether we can afford to embrace reciprocity but whether we can afford not to. The challenges of today's world—environmental degradation, social inequality, and economic volatility—demand a new approach to business. This approach sees businesses not as separate entities fighting for survival but as integral parts of a larger ecosystem, where success is measured not just by profit margins but by the positive impact we create.

In closing this section, I invite you, the reader, to reflect on the role of reciprocity in your own business journey. Consider the legacy you want to leave, not just for your company but for the world at large. The path of reciprocity is one of growth, resilience, and meaningful impact. It's a path leading to a future where businesses are celebrated for their success and contribution to a better world.

As we move forward to the conclusion of this chapter, let's carry with us the stories of Patagonia and other businesses that have illuminated the way. Let these stories inspire us to envision a new horizon for our businesses, one where growth is fueled by generosity, sustainability, and a deep commitment to the well-being of all. Together, let's embark on this journey of transformation guided by the enduring power of reciprocity.

## Conclusion and Action Steps

As we draw the curtains on this chapter, it's important to reflect on the journey we've embarked upon together. We've traversed the terrain of reciprocity, exploring its profound impact on sustainable business growth and the invaluable lessons it offers. Through stories of personal experiences, industry giants like Patagonia, and the myriad ways in which businesses can weave the golden thread of reciprocity into their very fabric, we've seen a new paradigm of business success unfold—one that is not just about profit, but about purpose, not just about transactions, but about transformation.

This chapter wasn't just a narrative but a call to action—a beckoning towards a future where businesses operate as stewards of society and the environment, where the principles of giving, sharing, and mutual respect are not just practiced but are pivotal to business strategy. The stories shared, the insights offered, and the examples cited were all aimed at illustrating one undeniable truth: that the path to lasting business success and growth is paved with the stones of reciprocity.

Now, as we stand at the threshold of this new dawn, it's time to look ahead and contemplate the next steps. How can we, as leaders, entrepreneurs, and change-makers, apply what we've learned to our ventures? How can we transform these insights into actionable strategies that propel our businesses forward and contribute to the greater good?

1. **Embrace Transparency:** Begin by fostering a culture of openness and transparency within your organization. Let your stakeholders know your commitments, challenges, and progress. This will build trust and lay the groundwork for reciprocal relationships.

2. **Invest in Relationships:** View every interaction with customers, employees, suppliers, and the community as an opportunity to build lasting relationships. Go beyond the transactional and seek to understand and meet their needs and values.

3. **Prioritize Sustainability:** Integrate sustainability into your business model. This isn't just about environmental sustainability but also about creating sustainable value for all your stakeholders. Initiatives like reducing waste, supporting local communities, and ensuring fair labor practices are all steps in the right direction.

4. **Encourage Participation:** Create avenues for your stakeholders to participate in your journey. Whether through feedback mechanisms, community

engagement programs, or collaborative projects, ensure they have a voice and a stake in your success.

5. **Measure Impact:** Finally, develop metrics to measure the impact of your reciprocity-based initiatives. This goes beyond financial performance to include social and environmental impact. Let these metrics guide your decisions and strategies.

As I pen these closing thoughts, I do so with optimism and a belief in the transformative power of reciprocity. Integrating these principles into our businesses is indeed a challenging one, fraught with uncertainties and requiring a leap of faith. Yet, it promises not just economic rewards but a deeper sense of fulfillment and purpose.

Let us not be daunted by the scale of the task ahead. Instead, let us draw inspiration from the success stories that light our path, the principles that ground us, and the vision of a world where businesses are a force for good. It's an achievable vision, one step at a time, one decision at a time, one act of reciprocity at a time.

As we conclude this chapter, I hope that you feel inspired to dream of a better future and act toward creating it. When woven into the fabric of our businesses, the principles of reciprocity can transform not just our companies but the world at large. It's a journey worth embarking on, and I invite you to join me. Together, let's pave the way for a new era of business—one marked by sustainability, growth, and mutual prosperity. Let's make reciprocity a chapter in our story and the essence of our legacy.

www.ingramcontent.com/pod-product-compliance
Lightning Source LLC
Chambersburg PA
CBHW060506130626
46553CB00002B/420